THE SULTAN OF SWAGGER

Leyritz brims with confide[nce]

HE'S got a wide-brimmed Stetson hanging in his locker
one. He wears cowboy hats everywhere.
"Aw, that's a little one," says Jim Leyritz. "I got bigger on[es]

Leyrit[z]

By MICHAEL EISEN

Like many m[en]
ers, Jim L[eyritz]

...all, Leyritz complained about
... and once, in a partic-
"a Pete Rose-
season, but

Montreal, Showalter was suggesting that Leyritz
help as a backup. And when trade talks fell throu[gh]
on the opening-day roster, the manager made
the facts of baseball life to him.

"Buck told me what he expected from
last night's series finale against the Seat[tle]
dome. "He told me I'd be a backup c[atcher]
...mes as a DH or infielder. He told me
... to me to take advantage
...cluded
Pat K[...]
home

Leyrit[z turns] into a happy Buckaroo

Merrill couldn['t]
not playing, didn[...]
ularly memora[ble]
type player." [...]
he almost cer[...]

Showal[ter]
Fort Laud[erdale]
with the [...]
me, [...]
...who [...]

During spring training, Buck Showalter repeat-
...value of versatility, the importance of having use-
bench who would be ready to follow through with

By MOSS KLEIN

...the players the Yankees manager had in mind was Jim
...he had doubts about him – with good reason. He
... year, Leyritz became a rebel with too many flaws. He
...between the Yankees and Columbus, sulking all the way.

Jim Leyritz
Won't Play
The Crying Game

by Tom Bannon

Three years ago he was one of the [...]
Albany, N.Y., W[ednesday...]

big
[...]t for A-C[...]

By Paul Schwartz
Staff writer

...LENS FALLS — How tough is Jim
...ritz?

...s tough as this: The day after being
...in the face by a pitch, he wanted to
...y again.

...So, it should come as no surprise that
...yritz was able to ignore the harsh
...nditions around him and lead ...
...on and ... Saturday after-

...ritz still lo[...]

Tirado halts Pittsfield in re[...]
Leyritz drives in winning r[un]

By Paul Schwartz
Staff writer

PITTSFIELD, Mass. — Aris Tirado
was the reason the Albany-Colonie
Yankees had to spend an extra hour in
the freezing cold Tuesday night.

Yet it was Tirado whose hand was
being slapped following Albany's 12-
inning, 5-4 Eastern League victory
over the Pittsfield Cubs.

Contradiction? Hardly. Tirado
pitched six innings of one-hit, shutout
relief. If not for the diminutive right-
hander, Jim Leyritz wouldn't have
been able to drive in the winning run
with a line single in the top of the 12th.
... doing my job," Tirado said.

...pitcher Kris Roth and then stole
second — the last of four Albany steals.
Leyritz, who is quickly earning the
reputation of being a clutch hitter,
drilled a 3-2 pitch into right-center
field for the game-winning run.

"The book on him was a big RBI
man, a tough hitter with two strikes,"
Jones said.

Dana Ridenour got the Yankees
back to the relative warmth of their
team bus by striking out the side in the
bottom of the 12th.

"That's the coldest I've ever been
while involved in a baseball game,"
Jones said, "but a good win will warm
you up quickly."

Pitching in near-freezing conditions
... or done," said Buck
... respect that."

...there. Just hold [...]
...dence we're going [...]

He couldn't ha[...]
...be so hard to com[...]

After a perfec[t...]
...a double to Jer[...]
...then retired 10 [...]
10th was succ[...]
play.

In the 11th, [...]
second basema[n...]
Ray Thoma [...]
told him (Sta[...]
let's go," Ti[...]
pressure on [...]
give up the r[...]

He struck [...]
third time to [...]
and star[...]
platoon [...]
a wave [...]

four years.
...een accept[...]
...ice feeling [...]
Indeed, [...]
...still annoy[...]
an issue an[...]
and he seer[...]
of the boys [...]
...le Davi[d...]
...by a slider [...]
...aken to M[...]
...er I[...]

Y., Sunday, April 1[...]

n the [...]

everyone'[...]

Leyrit[...]
ankees [...]
aroun[...]

Yan[...]
ba[...]

By JENNI[...]
New York

NEW [...]
made [...]
Leyritz [...]
Leyrit[z...]
tions.

D-6 THE TIMES UNION

"Jimmy has never shied [a]way from the ramifica[t]ions of anything he's said [o]r done," said Buck [S]howalter. "I respect that."

Leyritz, 29, has at-tempted this season to temper his behavior. He still shimmies his hips and twirls his bat between every pitch...

the season. This after he needed to hit .379 to merely make the team in spring and start the season as a platoon DH.

A wave of Yankee injuries struck. Showalter installed Leyritz as the cleanup hitter when Danny Tartabull went down. In the nine games since, a span in which the...

z oozes with confi[dence]

Torey Lovullo got a ticket to the Bronx before the cowboy. Leyritz wasn't going anywhere. So he opened that mouth again. And the Yankees suspended him. "They tried to make me invis-ible," says Jim Leyritz. But he...

[about guys promoted got to the [?]z swag-[?]um. He [?]vening. [?]ke the [?]g on as if he...

night long."
And think a[bout] one wrong.
Jim Leyritz

Leyritz Puts His Bat W[?]

By JENNIFER FREY

The day he made the major leagues, Jim Leyritz called his father. Don Leyritz did not say congratula-tions. He did not say, "I'm proud of you." He told his son, succinctly, "to go out there and do something." He expected him to make an immediate impact, he expected him to produce.

TIMES UNION ***

A-C's opener wo[n]

By Paul Schwartz
Staff writer

It's always fu[n]
...with a triple

Leyritz swings, he puts hurt on opp[?]

[?]RTY   lot of teams he could walk in and
long-ter[m]...start on."
[?]as hard for Le[yritz]
He wanted h[im]
[im]mediately, [?]
[h]imself, perha[ps]
[?]r. Either wa[y]
[?]n patience w[?]
[?]ires young players to...
wait their turn.

[J]immy's been here awhile Showalter said. "He's [establi]shed himself as a guy capa[ble] of helping the club. He's a [?] worker. He's certainly [ear]ned the respect of his peers. [An]d I think he's matured some."

Before the 1992 sea[son]
[i]n which Leyritz...

swagger, he still wears designer sun-glasses and brims with self-confi-dence. But that does not bother the Yankees because he has earned their respect. The proof is in the numbers that easily back Leyritz's self-promo[tion]

[?]ro reco[rd]

"I think they respect h[im?]
[?]er," said Buck Showalter
[?]aged Leyritz [?]
[?]onta in [?]

	12	23	0
66	111	2
37	70	0

By Paul Schwartz
Staff writer

COLONIE — The Albany-Colonie Yankee[s]
services of catcher Jim Ley[ritz?]
beaned by Pittsfield [?]
Leyritz wa[s]
in the sixth inn[ing]
and needed six...

[?]ting day marred b[y]

plate, le[?]

Leyritz gets big hit for A-[C]

By Paul Schwartz
Staff writer

GLENS FALLS — How toug[h is] Leyritz?

As tough as this: The day aft[er being] hit in the face by a pitch, he w[anted to] play again.

So, it should come a[?]
Leyritz wa[s]
suddenly condi[?]
becaus[e]

Four Named To Leagu[e]

Four Forest Hills bas-keteers have been named to the American Division All-Star Basketball first [?] a fifth made

[?]ilton County Suburban Athletic Association.
Anderson senior Joe[?]
Deeds, Anderson juniors [?]
Tim Ferguson and Jo[e]

Turpin Cat[ches?]

BY MICHAEL PAOLERCIO
Sports Reporter

A little book-learning can go a long way. Just ask Jim Leyritz.
The Turpin catcher entered this week [?]first among the city's batting leaders [with a] .000, .714 average (20 of 28 at bat)

Leyri[tz]

By Paul Sch[wartz]
Staff writer

PITTSFIELD [?]
was the reaso[n]
Yankees had to s[?]
the freezing col[d]
Yet it was T[?]
being slapped [?]
inning, 5-4 E[?]
over the Pittsf[ield]

Contradict[?]
pitched six in[?]
relief. If not [?]
[h]ander, Jim [?]
been able to [?]
with a line si[?]
Just doin[g]

Leyritz t[?]

By MOSS KLEIN

SEATTLE — During spring training, Buck Showalter repeat-[e]dly discussed the value of versatility, the importance of having use-[f]ul players on the bench who would be ready to follow through with [h]is maneuvers.
Among the players the Yankees manager had in mind was Jim [L]eyritz, but he had doubts about him — with good reason. He [?]bel with too many flaws. He

Merrill could[n't?]
not playing, didn't per[form?]
[p]ularly memorable statement [?]
type player." Merrill was cri[tical?]
he almost certainly wouldn't [?]

Showalter, who was Ley[ritz's?]
Fort Lauderdale in 1987 and [?]
with the temperamental play[er?]
me, he has seen my ups and my downs[.]
While the Yankees were attemptin[g]

[?]ees

TIMES UNION ***

the wait [?]
OF S[?]

[i]ury
[?]mor-[?]
[?]te. While
[?]y confid[ent]
[?]ver lip.
His
[?]ner players
[?]ones
[?]e things w[?]
[?]t he talks p[?]

D-8   SUND[AY]

CATCHING
HEAT

THE
JIM
LEYRITZ
STORY

JIM LEYRITZ
DOUGLAS B. LYONS
& JEFFREY LYONS

Health Communications, Inc.
Deerfield Beach, Florida

www.hcibooks.com

Library of Congress Cataloging-in-Publication Data

Leyritz, Jim.
Catching heat : the Jim Leyritz story / Jim Leyritz, Douglas B. Lyons
    & Jeffrey Lyons.
        p. cm.
    ISBN-13: 978-0-7573-1566-4 (hardcover)
    ISBN-10: 0-7573-1566-6 (hardcover)
    ISBN-13: 978-0-7573-9185-9 (e-book)
    ISBN-10: 0-7573-9185-0 (e-book)
    1. Leyritz, Jim.   2. Baseball players—United States—Biography.   3.
Catchers
        (Baseball)—United States—Biography.   I. Lyons, Douglas B. II.
Lyons, Jeffrey.
        III. Title.
    GV865.L49A3 2011
    796.357092--dc22
    [B]
                                                                    2011013915

Publisher: Health Communications, Inc.
            3201 S.W. 15th Street
            Deerfield Beach, FL 33442–8190

Cover design by Justin Rotkowitz
Interior design and formatting by Dawn Von Strolley Grove

In Memory of
Joe Toerner

Contents

Introduction

Imagine you're just moments away from reaching your childhood dream. All that stands between you and your life-defining goal is ticking seconds on a clock. Suddenly, your entire life is about to change forever.

For some, the moment that leads them to their destiny happens because they make an instinctive decision, or meet the right person at the right time, or strategically plan for it day in and day out. For me, all of my dreams came true with one swing of a bat.

My defining moment came on October 23, 1996, in front of 52,000 fans at Atlanta-Fulton County Stadium while millions more watched on TV around the world. That swing, which ultimately resulted in a World Series turnaround and win for the New York Yankees against the Atlanta Braves, was the culmination of twenty-five years of sacrifice, hardship, injury, betrayal, failure, success, decisions right and wrong, hard work, and a lot of sweat.

My life-long dream of being part of an historic baseball moment had finally been fulfilled. But at what cost? Sometimes I had to sacrifice my relationships and my beliefs to reach my ticker-tape moment. When you achieve lofty goals at such a young age, something scary happens after the storm of media and excitement passes. After the word "hero" is tacked onto your name, the calm settles in, and the phone calls quiet down. You sit and find yourself asking, *Now what?* What you have worked for all your life has defined you, and now you've hit the big time, so you ask yourself, *What's next? What defines me now? What do I work toward next? What is to come, and how will I get there?*

With that swing, I'd achieved every personal goal I'd set for myself as a young man. Now, every Yankee fan would remember that homerun and the name that went with it. I had lived my dream. But I'd become tricked into thinking that somehow, because so many wonderful things happened to me in such a short amount of time, my fortune would continue. Little did I know that my life and struggles were just beginning. The results would not always garner ticker tape. Different paths would have to be taken. Some bumpy, some straight.

It's said that once at the top, there's only one way to go—down. I learned the hard way what that means and that the direction was downward. Some of the mistakes which led to my descent were of my own doing, and some, I believe, were the doings of others. All were brought to me from a higher power, as humbling reminders that I'm not so special or perfect and that I need to pay better attention to the values and morals my parents instilled in me. Otherwise, it can all be taken away.

Every time I started to believe *I* was in control, that *I* created my plan or destiny, God found a way to remind me: stay grounded. Your plans have already been made. And the 1996 home run was *not* a destination, just part of the journey that I'm still on to this day.

Through this book, I invite you on this journey of dreams that came true, tragedies which tested my faith, and triumphs that would once again give me the spirit of hope. I want to share with you how I learned the hard way that life is a succession of mountainous climbs: each mountain is put in our path to teach us how to climb better and more efficiently the next, with hope, faith, and happiness revealed along the way.

Most people remember me for two events, both of which tested my faith in different ways. I controlled one. The other, I did not. I was in control of the home run I hit in the 1996 World Series against the Atlanta Braves, which turned the Series around for the New York Yankees and eventually led them to the World Championship.

I was *not* in control of the 2007 car accident in which I was involved and resulted in the tragic loss of a woman's life.

Through God's love, I decided that I would not let my life be defined by either of these moments.

This is my story.

1

A Family Affair

Before reaching the major leagues, I'd broken my hand, foot, wrist, finger, arm, and leg, blown out my knee, torn a ligament in my ankle, and been hit in the face with a pitch. I even had surgery on my left knee, which still gives me trouble. But, by June of 1990, I was wearing a New York Yankees uniform in the major leagues.

I was never your typical ballplayer and had never

followed the predictable path to success. The typical player gets drafted after junior college or college, or occasionally right out of high school. Then he plays his way up through the minors, progressing from rookie ball, through A ball, AA, AAA, and finally being called up to the big-league club. Even a great pitcher like Ron Guidry spent ten years in the minors, honing his skills, working his way up to the major leagues. A few make it. Most don't. The odds of a player being drafted and playing eleven years in the major leagues are slim to none.

But in 1996, the Yankees magical season, I was the most tenured player on the team. I believed hard work and faith, rather than pure talent, was the way to make the major leagues. My path was living proof that setting dreams and goals to strive for was the first step to achieving success. But hard work, commitment, and faith all had to come together to make these goals and dreams come true.

At just six feet and 195 pounds, I was not very big by major-league standards. Also, more ballplayers come from California than any other state, but I grew up in Cincinnati, Ohio. In California, Florida, Arizona, and Texas kids can play baseball all year round, but not in Ohio. Nevertheless, my career as a professional baseball player was inevitable, no matter how many other talented players came before or after me.

My first seven years with the Yankees were a battle. I wanted more playing time, or better yet, just one season—

one chance of being an everyday player. They kept telling me to be patient. But every year, it was the same: just 250–260 at bats as a part-time player. An everyday player usually gets 500–600 at bats per season. I was always the Kramer to somebody else's Seinfeld. They told me to see the forest through the trees, but I was young and wanted to be given a chance to be a regular. The Yankees kept telling me that I was more valuable off the bench—but the bench didn't pay the bills.

Tenacity over talent was my motto, and I am a living, breathing example of the truth behind this philosophy. What I didn't know was that my determination to become a pro athlete, plus my faith and hard work, would become vital in the other parts of my life. That drive is what has kept me going through the good times and the bad in my career, love life, family, and even with the justice system. And, man, there have been challenges in all of those areas.

I've been no stranger to adversity throughout my career. I've had my ups and downs—with the Yankees on three different occasions, the Anaheim Angels, the Texas Rangers, the Boston Red Sox, the San Diego Padres, and briefly, the Los Angeles Dodgers. I've had mostly ups, but when there were downs, they were doozies. Most of my arguments in baseball were not with umpires, despite my squatting in front of them during the eleven years I caught, but with managers and general managers, and usually over the same thing: I wanted more playing time.

No matter the team, I always thought I'd earned a full-time slot on the roster. They usually didn't agree with me. It seemed I was always fighting for my right to be front and center, but there was this overwhelming and pestering consensus that I was a backup.

I've also had my ups and downs in my personal life: two failed marriages, with one resulting in a hard-fought award of primary custody of my three children; my youngest son battling two serious illnesses before he was nine months old; and the decision to give up the game I loved to become a full-time father in 2003.

Then, most recently, on my forty-fourth birthday on December 27, 2007, I was involved in a car accident that resulted in the death of a young woman. I was charged with two counts: driving under the influence of alcohol and vehicular manslaughter. I had asserted from the beginning that I was not responsible for the accident, but it took me three painstaking years to prove my innocence. The trial took another eighteen nerve-racking days. I was acquitted of vehicular manslaughter (a felony that could have sent me to prison for fifteen years) and instead convicted of a charge that my attorney and I had told the state that I'd plead to from the beginning: a DUI as a first-time offense, a valuable lesson that drinking and driving can be very costly to anyone who does it.

I had faith that things would work out and that I would be vindicated, just as I had faith in high school and in college that my career would take off, despite being skipped by the draft three times; just as I knew that I would get the playing time I deserved; and just as I had when it seemed that I was losing my family and the chance to be a first-rate dad.

My proudest achievements are when I retired from baseball to become the type of father my mom and dad were proud of—and when I achieved what I had always dreamed of: an eleven-year major-league career that included playing on three different teams in three different World Series. I also had one memorable moment that most young men only dream of: a chance to contribute one of the most important turning points in World Series history as a New York Yankee in Game 4 of the 1996 Series.

My parents, Don and Betty, met while attending Kent State University. Both were very athletic. My father played basketball, and my mother was a physical education major. Dad graduated in June 1956. They married in July in Cleveland and by September, he was drafted into the U.S. Army. After he completed his military duty they returned and settled in Cleveland.

Dad began working as a salesman for IBM, and they eventually started a family. My older brother Mike was born on August 21, 1959. Mike was the best athlete in our family. He had more natural ability than I could ever dream of. We used to have some great one-on-one basketball games in our driveway. When I was younger, he always used to win. (He was two inches taller.) As I got bigger and stronger, I beat him a few times. But Mike would always say that he *let* me win.

My parents always made Mike take me along when he went to do anything sports-related with his friends. I know he must have hated it, but I was a pretty good athlete even as a little kid, and I could hold my own against older, bigger kids. Mike may not have realized it, but he was instrumental in my becoming a professional athlete.

The constant challenges in competition gave me the confidence that I'd need later to make it as a pro baseball player. I don't know if I've ever told him, but I owe my brother Mike a big thank-you. Today, Mike and his wife Nancy are the proud parents of two beautiful daughters: Stephanie (twenty-one) and Alyssa (nineteen), who are both in college.

My sister, Lori, was born on May 5, 1961. She was also a very good athlete and played soccer during high school. Lori was not a typical "girlie-girl." She wasn't interested in ballet or modern dance and instead preferred playing sports or watching them. Mike and I never realized how lucky we were to have a sister who didn't keep us from doing some of the things we wanted to do athletically. Lori was happier watching a football or basketball game on TV or in person than shopping at a mall with her girl-friends. I owe my sister Lori a big thank-you, for she also enabled me to pursue my career. Lori and her husband, my late brother-in-law Joe Toerner (who passed away in August 2010 from ALS/Lou Gehrig's disease), have two boys, Zach (nineteen) and Matt (sixteen). Zach may be following his Uncle Jim's path to professional baseball. He plays for Northern Kentucky University. Matt is a high-school sophomore on the varsity football team for Hamilton-Badin in Hamilton, Ohio.

As a physical-education major in college, my mom knew a lot about sports. Not too many kids whose fathers were working could go out in their backyards and have a good catch with their mothers. I could. My mom worked with me on my throwing and my catching techniques. I always joked with my dad that I knew where I got my athletic ability from, and it wasn't from him. Like most mothers, my mom was always there to pick me up when I was down. She always encouraged me to keep trying, even when I failed. She was my rock. Without her support and guidance, I could not have made it through my life as a professional athlete, or through some of the tough personal difficulties that I faced later in life.

My dad was my coach, mentor, and role model. He

held me to my word: if you promised him something, you better deliver. If you said something, be ready to back it up. He knew I wouldn't always agree with my coaches and managers. He wanted to prepare me for the inevitable conflicts that would arise when someone challenged me. He always used to say, "If you do something, do it with conviction. Never walk away knowing you didn't give your best effort." My dad made many sacrifices for his family, especially for me. He held firmly to his faith, and his beliefs formed the strong foundation for my own.

Yet as solid as he was on the exterior, he had a soft side too, which few people outside of our family ever saw. He made decisions that he knew were in the family's best interests. His decisions and actions were selfless. Dad was a hardworking, hard-driving man, and the main reason I was able to fulfill my dream of becoming a professional athlete. He rarely said, "I love you," but his actions showed us time and again how much he did. Today, I'm the proud father of three boys: Austin (sixteen), Dakota (fourteen), and Phoenix (ten). I hope to pass on to them the same values I learned from my parents: hard work, determination, faith, perseverance, and honesty.

As a family, we were all very athletic. In our house, if the TV was on, somebody was watching sports. If we weren't watching sports, we would usually be out playing them. We were very competitive, even with each other. Most of our family vacations centered on sports. We spent most spring break vacations making the seventeen-hour drive to Tampa for spring training to watch the Reds prepare for the upcoming baseball season.

We were very lucky to have the four major pro sports teams in Cincinnati. In addition to the Reds we had the NFL Bengals, the WHA Stingers (hockey), and the ABA Cincinnati Royals (later the Sacramento Kings in the NBA). If we didn't go to the games, we watched them on TV or listened on the radio. In our lives, sports were a family affair. We all supported one another. My mom and dad still regularly play golf and watch sports on TV every day, unless they're at one of their grandchildren's games or recitals.

The youngest in the family, I was born in Lakewood, Ohio, on December 27, 1963. In 1970, when I was six, my family moved to Cincinnati when my father was transferred. When I was ten, one of my Little League teammates was a kid named Thom Brennaman. Thom's dad, Marty, was a broadcaster for the Cincinnati Reds. As Thom and I became better friends, our families got to know each other.

One year, Marty invited my family to Tampa during our two-week spring break to stay at the Reds' team hotel and watch the team in spring training. Since all of us were sports addicts, we jumped at the opportunity. This was how we wanted to spend our spring break. How many kids have the opportunity not only to meet their childhood heroes but to stay at the same hotel with them and their families? While our families basked by the hotel pool, Thom and I went to the ballpark with Marty. We got to be ball boys on occasion and got to go into the dugout, the clubhouse, and on the field where the players worked out. What a thrill!

One day on one of the other fields, a camera crew was setting up. Former Notre Dame football coach Ara Parseghian was in Tampa to film a segment on the Cincinnati Reds for his TV show about the proper techniques for hitting and catching. Pete Rose would do the hitting and Johnny Bench the catching. The producers were looking for two kids to help with the demonstration. Guess who?

Rose said, "Tommy, you do the hitting with me. Jimmy, you do the catching with Johnny." I was so nervous—here I was playing catch with the great Johnny Bench, a future Hall of Famer! He demonstrated proper positioning for receiving the ball, how to throw down to second base, and the footwork required for both. After the filming ended, Bench handed me his catcher's mitt and a ball. I couldn't believe it! *I was holding Johnny Bench's actual catcher's mitt*! I found my dad and showed it to him. "Dad, I'm going to be a catcher!" I exclaimed. That day changed my life. Johnny Bench probably didn't realize at the time what an influence he had on my decision to become a catcher. Years later, we met at an autograph-signing event where I thanked him for being my inspiration.

For the next few years, our family made the same seven-teen-hour drive to Tampa to see the Reds, creating more great memories. Thom and I were ball boys for George Foster and Ken Griffey Sr. while they played tennis on the hotel court. I remember playing Pac-Man (then the cutting-edge of video games) with Davey Concepción in the hotel lobby. All of these experiences became integral factors in the decision I would make years later when choosing whether to play baseball or basketball.

Thom and I remain close friends to this day. He has joined Marty (now a Hall of Fame broadcaster) to announce Reds games. Maybe one day, when Marty decides to retire, I'll join Thom in the Reds radio booth!

When I was growing up in Cincinnati and spending time with the Reds, Pete Rose became my idol. While he wasn't the most naturally gifted player on the team, he made himself into a great ballplayer by working harder than anyone else. I watched how he worked and tried to copy his approach. Pete's fierce determination and grit made up for his lack of natural ability. I related to this since I was never the most talented athlete—even in my own family. That position was held by my brother Mike, who is four years older. When Mike was in high school, our dad tried to coach and push him. But Mike made it clear to our dad that he didn't want him to be his coach. He already had a coach. He just wanted Dad to sit, watch, and be a dad.

Mike wasn't planning to be a professional athlete like I was, so our father focused his coaching efforts on me. I told my dad that I wanted to be a college athlete, and hopefully a pro, though I hadn't yet decided between basketball and baseball. I wanted him to challenge me, to push me to do better in sports and in my studies. I thrived on that type of coaching. With my father officially dedicated to my goal of becoming a baseball or basketball player in college, and later, perhaps, a professional, he developed a coaching style that he thought I could handle—a tough, no excuses approach based on accountability, purpose, and lots of sweat. He was from the old school. I would describe this approach as Dad channeling his favorite coaches, Hall of Famers Bobby Knight and Woody Hayes.

Knight was the maniacal basketball coach at Indiana University (1971–2000) who verbally abused his own players and his critics. But his teams won. Hayes was the football coach at Ohio State (1951–78). He coached in the same style—anything to drive his team to win. I know my father loved coaching me. It was a welcome reprieve from his day job.

My parents began to focus on helping me get an athletic scholarship to college. They believed I could do it and knew that it would require tremendous effort and discipline. This is when my family began to make sacrifices on my behalf, sometimes at the expense of the other members of our family. My mom, Betty, was in charge of

Mike, Lori, and me to all of our games and prac-
ad frequently left work early and tried never to
of our games. What my parents sacrificed in the
sports for their children is truly remarkable. Dad
opportunities to transfer and take better jobs
for more money, but he knew it would disrupt
so he didn't take them.

y parents gave up a lot on my behalf, so did
ike. The time and effort our parents took to
d the country to get me to all my baseball and
mes took away from things Mike and Lori
When I got my first professional contract,
i must have felt relieved that the sacrifices
for me to become a pro athlete had finally

now concentrating solely on my athletic
d me—hard. His extreme tough-as-nails
pt me focused and got the most out of
of my teammates' parents felt my father
o hard. One of the other fathers asked
ght that my father was too hard on me.
d asked my father to stay on me." He
a coach could. If I went three-for-four
fo ed to know why it hadn't been *four-*
he thirty points in a basketball game,
ha vhy not thirty-*five*? This may sound
it and it worked; he helped make

me a better athlete and a better person.

He'd often yell instructions from behind the benc
during my basketball games. (His instructions were on
directed at me, never at my teammates.) Sometimes]
yell back, asking him to be quiet. Yet his instructions w
usually right, telling me when to shoot or pass the b
Once, I was about thirty feet from the basket and I h
tated. Then I heard him yell, "Shoot!" I shot and I m
it! He seemed to know me better than I knew myself.

Occasionally, the coach and the school would
upset about his antics. Once, without my knowledge
banished him to the upstairs bleachers. When I l
into the stands where he usually sat, he wasn't the
I could still hear him yelling at me. After the gan
mother told me that he had been asked to move t
he was bothering the coach. When I learned of
walked into the principal's office and threw my
ball uniform on his desk. I told him that if th
going to treat my father this way, I'd quit the tear
next game, my dad was back behind the bench
toned down his yelling a little. But every now
undaunted, he would continue to shout instr
me. He'd played basketball at Kent State Unive
1950s, so I trusted his instincts.

Baseball was a different story. Dad didn't
much about the game, so he didn't shout ins
much as he'd done on the basketball court.]

thought it was needed, he'd yell. His criticism was more general, about hustling and giving 100 percent, not specific play instructions. This type of motivation worked for me and gave me the strength and fortitude never to be satisfied unless I tried my best. I continued to work hard every day. Dad believed in the adage, "You're only as good as your last performance." Sure, I was blessed with some athletic ability, but ambition, drive, determination, and good coaching propelled me to the top.

I had played basketball, football, and baseball while growing up, and by the time I got to high school, the days and nights of constant drills, the high expectations, and the repetitive workouts began paying off. I was the golden boy, the star athlete—except in football. I dropped football after the eighth grade because I broke my left hand and was forced to miss half the basketball season. Basketball was my favorite sport. There was no way I was going to risk a serious injury in a sport I didn't like. So, once I entered high school, I switched from football to golf and quickly made the varsity team as a sophomore.

As advanced as I was athletically, emotionally I was not on the same emotional level as the more mature juniors and seniors on my various teams. I looked up to them, but I didn't want to socialize with them too much. Many times there was a lot of peer pressure on me to join in. This caused me many difficult moments. High school was challenging enough, and playing on teams with kids who were two or three years older made for some uncomfortable situations. The older guys were going out with girls and experimenting with things that seventeen and eighteen-year-olds sometimes do—but not fifteen-year-olds. I knew God's presence was guiding me to do the right thing and stay focused on sports. It didn't always make me the most popular guy on the team, but I felt that not joining them was the right thing to do.

My family attended Anderson Township Methodist Church almost every Sunday. I went to Bible class on Wednesday nights, mostly so I could play basketball. For the first hour we learned about God, but afterward we were dismissed to go to the gym and play basketball. It was a pretty smart move on the church's part, as I never missed a class! My parents were churchgoers who taught me that church was a place where I could seek answers and get shelter from everyday life, a safe haven where I could pray for the things that I wanted most; not material things, but spiritual guidance and direction toward achieving my goals, which sometimes seemed unattainable. During the beginning of the services, I'd often try to figure out what message the pastor would use to illustrate the Gospel and then make up my own anecdote that I wished he would use so we could apply the messages to our everyday lives.

I was brought up to believe that to be a great athlete, you had to be special; you didn't drink or smoke, and you definitely stayed out of trouble. If you wanted to be on the high school athletic teams, you also had to get good grades. Instead of going out to parties with everyone, I'd practice shooting baskets in my driveway or hitting baseballs in the basement. During high school I took a job at a batting cage just so I could hit as much as I wanted to for free when business was slow.

Often when I told my friends that I was going to be a professional athlete, they laughed and told me I'd never make it, that I was missing out on having fun with them. But I was undeterred. From the tenth grade on, I practiced signing my autograph until it was perfect. I didn't know which sport would be my ticket to stardom, but I knew I would be a pro, and I wanted my autograph to be special.

In tenth grade I started to date a girl named Christy, and our relationship lasted through the end of high school. It was a cliché match: star athlete dating the popular cheerleader. We were in love and believed that we would get married one day. After high school, we tried to continue dating, but the distance was too much. She was at Miami University in Oxford, Ohio, and I went to Middle Georgia Junior College. The twelve-hour drive to see each other began to interfere with my schoolwork, practices, and games. Breaking up with Christy would be the first of many heartbreaks and relationship sacrifices that I would have to make while pursuing my baseball dreams.

2

Big League Dreams

In 1981, during my junior year of high school, the scouts—college and pro—came to watch me play. My dad saw them taking notes; they knew I could hit and catch. I had an excellent batting eye and some speed, too. I wore number 14, honoring my idol Pete Rose. My father told me that the scouts were watching every move I made on the field, so I needed to hustle and run out every ball, no matter how poorly I may have hit it. They'd notice if I slammed my helmet down after striking out. They'd also study my mechanics behind the plate, how I framed pitches, reacted to foul pop-ups, and how quickly I got the ball from home to second.

I had a great start that season, and one newspaper ranked me one of the top five high school players in all of Cincinnati. Barry Larkin, my good friend and summer league teammate (and, I hope, a future Hall of Famer) was ranked the best player in the city. Despite knowing that the scouts were watching, I never felt any added pressure. I knew there was no other place this road was going to lead than to the major leagues; it was just a matter of time.

I finished my junior year of high school and was receiving scholarship offers from a number of colleges for basketball and baseball. Basketball was still my number one passion. I could shoot and dribble. I compared myself to Kyle Macy of the University of Kentucky and later the Phoenix Suns, Chicago Bulls, and Indianapolis Pacers of the NBA. I liked his skills and his style of play. I even imitated his habit of bouncing the ball five times at the free-throw line. But he was six feet three inches tall.

Our Turpin High School basketball team went to the regional finals in Cincinnati that year. We had upset Taft, the top-seeded school in the tournament, but we'd lost to Western Hills in the finals. I had scored a career-high thirty-three points against Taft, but was continually double-teamed and held to just ten in my final game.

Dad and I spoke about my future in sports, whether I should pursue basketball or baseball. He said I had a choice: I could be a good college basketball player, or perhaps a major-league baseball player. I realized that at just five feet ten inches and 165 pounds, my best chance of being a professional athlete was in baseball. The average NBA player is more than half a foot taller. People don't want college players' autographs. So I chose to concentrate on baseball.

During my senior year, I still played basketball and led the Turpin Spartans in scoring. But instead of staying late and shooting baskets, I went home. After finishing my homework, I'd go down to my basement to practice my baseball swing. I had an orange traffic cone that was the perfect height for a batting tee. I hung a sheet from the ceiling to catch the balls so I didn't break anything. Hour after hour, I hit an endless stream of tennis balls into that sheet. I thought about Pete Rose and the mental games he devised for himself—not just monotonously hitting ball after ball. Rose played mental games in spring training by imagining himself in different game situations—hit-and-run, man on third—concentrating on hitting line drives on every swing. I did the same for about two hours every night.

After basketball season ended in my senior year, it

was time to concentrate on baseball. I wanted to impress the scouts. I went 48/100 with just two strikeouts, still a Turpin High School record. The amateur draft was in June, when major-league teams rely on scouting reports of high school and college players. By then I'd started playing summer league ball for the Midland Redskins, a select travel team in the elite Connie Mack League, which is made up of the best high school players in town. If you were a good high school player in the Cincinnati area, you were going to play for Midland. In addition to playing in Ohio, we played games as far away as Kentucky and Tennessee. My roommate on the team was future Reds shortstop Barry Larkin. Todd Benzinger, another future major leaguer, was also a teammate. Other future stars who played for Midland were Rich Dotson, Ken Griffey Jr., and Tuffy Rhodes.

Joe Hayden was the owner of the team. "Poppa Joe" as we called him, was one of the classiest, most generous men I've ever known, similar to the man I'd later play for in the major leagues, George Steinbrenner. Like Steinbrenner, Hayden provided us with everything we needed to be successful, but it was up to *us* to perform on the field. He expected 100 percent effort at all times.

After I graduated from high school, we began practicing for the summer league. There was a break between the end of high school and the amateur baseball draft. Some of the scouts told my father that they were interested in me. They liked the way I hit: I hit for average and I had good power. I watched the ball into the catcher's mitt after every pitch. I ran to first base after a walk—all things that Pete Rose had taught me. They liked the way I carried myself on the field. I was confident and never backed down in any situation. They could tell that the bigger the situation, the bolder I got. I wanted that chance to drive in the winning run. During that time, my father was contacted by Hep Cronin, a scout for the Braves. He had begun to talk to my coaches too. My stock in the upcoming June draft seemed to be going up every day. I finished the high school year and made the Ohio All-State team, an honor I was very proud of.

After my senior year, a few of the pro scouts wanted to know whether I'd sign a pro contract or play college ball. My father told the scout to call him and make an offer when they got close to the draft. Now I could just sit back and see where I was going to be drafted and by whom. My dream was coming true. I couldn't wait for that phone call, with the voice on the other end saying, "You've been drafted by the . . ." Unfortunately, that call never came.

Two days before the draft, I decided to play tennis with my friend Todd Blaine. I had always joked with Todd, the top tennis player at Turpin High, that if baseball weren't played at the same time as tennis, *I'd* be the best player on the team. We decided to play a match that day to decide.

In the first set, I went up for a smash and landed awk-
wardly on my left foot. I felt something snap.

We drove to the hospital where x-rays revealed that I'd
fractured my foot, and I had to be put in a cast. I couldn't
believe it. During the whole drive home, I kept wondering
what I'd tell my parents. You can imagine their reaction
when I walked in with a cast on my left foot. Surprisingly,
my mother seemed to be more upset than my father. His
attitude, predictably, was "This is your mistake. You're the
one who has to live with it." My dad knew what this would
do to my chances of being drafted. Both of my parents were
disappointed, because I might have ruined my chances of
becoming a professional baseball player. But deep down, I
think they both wanted me to go to college first.

The next night, the scout called to say that the Braves
were thinking of drafting me. They wanted to know if
I would sign. My father told the scout that I wanted to
play professional baseball, and that I would definitely
sign. Then he conveyed the devastating news: "Unfortunately, Jim broke his foot yesterday playing tennis." I
knew that with my leg in a cast, I'd no longer be a top
pick. But I still expected to be drafted somewhere. After
all, I'd been an all-state player my senior year and was
playing for the Midland Redskins in the elite Connie
Mack League.

After I broke my foot, the scouts said that they would
continue to watch me play when I recovered, but they

weren't going to waste a draft pick on me in my condition. I was completely devastated. The draft had come and gone and no one had taken a chance on me. Still determined to become a pro ballplayer, the following week I asked my doctor to put a new brace on my foot so I could stay in shape and take batting practice with the Redskins. I was still trying to get a baseball scholarship to college and knew that by the end of the summer, I would be playing again.

After I learned that my future did not include a spot in the amateur draft, I realized my stock as a player was precarious, and I didn't want to be left behind. I continued to stay in shape and took batting practice every day, still sporting a cast on my ankle. I could walk on it, and still do some things—but definitely not everything. I couldn't bend it. I had to stay on my back foot, and that included when I batted. I continued to bat, but with my left leg stiff to keep the weight off it. Over time I became used to the new stance and started to develop more power. After the cast came off six weeks later, in mid-July, I never changed my stance. That batting stance would later help propel me to the big leagues. But clearly, becoming a professional athlete would be on God's time, not mine.

— ~ —

I wore uniform number 14 in high school and college—just like Pete Rose. After I graduated, Turpin High School retired it. When I finally made the Yankees, Lou Piniella, who wore number 14, had just been fired as manager, and Nick Priore, the clubhouse attendant, wouldn't give out number 14 just yet. So I wore number 12. In 1991, the Yankees sent me down to the minors and called Pat Kelly up to the Yankees. Fiore gave Kelly number 14. I was upset. When I got called back up, I tried to pull rank, and asked Kelly for number 14. He refused. So I never got number 14. I stayed with number 12.

In 1993, when Wade Boggs came to the Yankees, he wanted number 12. Our closer, Steve Farr, wore number 26, the number Boggs had worn in Boston. Boggs's seniority in terms of years of service (and five batting titles, including four in a row) entitled him to pick whatever uniform number he wanted. He wanted number 12, he got number 12. Farr had to choose a new number. By that time, Kelly had been wearing number 14 for two years, and I wasn't going to get that number. So I picked the closest number: number 13.

I had a great year in 1993 and again in 1994. The theory that the number 13 brings bad luck? I just didn't believe it. And I now joke that one day, the Yankees will retire my number because it's currently worn by Álex Rodríguez.

Things happen for a reason and there is always good that comes out of bad. My broken foot gave me a unique and instantly recognizable batting stance. It also forced me to learn to play different positions, which helped keep me in the big leagues for eleven years because managers love versatile utility players. I became a jack-of-all-trades, just like Pete Rose. He had been an all-star in left field, right field, at third base, and at first. During my major-league career, in addition to catching and occasionally being the designated hitter (DH), I played first, second, third, left field, and right field—every position except centerfield, shortstop, and pitcher. Many utility players can play different positions, but very few can catch. Elston Howard was a left fielder and a catcher. "Big" Cliff Johnson was a first baseman, an outfielder, and a catcher. Johnny Blanchard was a catcher and an outfielder. My ability to play so many different positions was an advantage to the team: with me on the roster, they could carry three catchers and have one fewer first baseman to make room for another pitcher or an outfielder. A team could easily decide to pinch-hit for the starting catcher (putting in Bob Geren or Matt Nokes, say, for the Yankees), knowing that I was available to catch.

When you think of unusual or instantly recognizable stances, there's Stan "the Man" Musial's corkscrew stance, Joe DiMaggio's feet-wide-apart stance, Mel Ott's foot-in-the-bucket stance, Rickey Henderson's pronounced crouch at the plate, Jay Buhner's straight-up stance, Carl Yastrzemski's hands-above-his-shoulders stance, and, more recently, Craig Counsell's straight up-and-down stance. If you saw these players only in silhouette, you'd still know who they were. The stiff-legged stance that my broken foot and cast forced me to adopt gave me one of those instantly recognizable stances too. I used to twirl my bat between pitches. I developed this habit not to be a showboat, but because we had all decided to do our trick during a game. After taking a pitch and doing the twirl, the next pitch I hit a home run, so I kept doing it.

— ~

Despite the setback of not being drafted, my parents were happy at the prospect of my attending college. They wanted me to further my education. Although my broken foot delayed my professional path and forced me to reassess my goals and plans, the major leagues were still my dream.

The scouts who had been watching me recommended to my parents that I go to a junior college. This way I'd be eligible for the draft after just one year of school, rather than having to wait three years at a four-year university. My parents and I decided a junior college would be my best route. They spoke to the scouts who suggested two schools for me: Indian River Community College in Fort Pierce on Florida's eastern coast, and Middle Georgia Junior College, a baseball school in the middle of nowhere: Cochran, Georgia. I was too busy playing summer baseball to look at schools myself. I trusted my parents' judgment; they knew what was best for me. My parents chose Middle Georgia for me. I hadn't even seen it before I went there.

My foot was not healed enough to permit me to put too much weight on it, so I couldn't catch just yet. I played third base and the outfield. I had what they call the "Bill Walton crack." A similar crack on Walton's foot had shortened his NBA career. The crack was on a part of the bone that could never fully heal. Twenty-eight years later, I still wake up some mornings with a shooting pain in my left foot.

At Middle Georgia there wasn't a whole lot to do except play baseball. There were only 300 students on campus and not much activity. I met a girl named Jennifer and we dated my entire freshman year. I always liked being in a relationship and enjoyed spending quiet time with one person, away from the crazy campus life. The following year, she transferred to the University of Georgia in Athens, one hundred miles away, and I stayed at Middle Georgia. The distance kept us apart and we eventually went separate ways. I didn't really have a girlfriend my second year and decided to play the field (no pun intended). I began having fewer relationships and more casual sex.

This no-commitment policy was new for me. At first, it was fun. Having the freedom to meet whoever I wanted whenever I wanted and not sticking to a specific "type" of woman boosted my ego. But after a while, it became monotonous. Never connecting or feeling a closeness or mutual respect with a woman started to feel empty. Ultimately, it wasn't who I was. I had enjoyed the relationships I had with Christy and Jennifer, which included healthy communication and the security of knowing that someone was invested in you and you in them, much like the marriage my parents had. Ultimately, while I could impress my friends with my "track record," it just didn't feel right to me morally.

During my first baseball season with the Warriors at Middle Georgia, I struck out only twice. In my second year, I was second in the league in hitting. Because of the good season I'd had, I thought I'd be drafted. For reasons I still cannot figure out, I wasn't. I focused on deciding which four-year college to attend, and my decision was heavily influenced by which school was known for its baseball. I knew that the University of Kentucky in Lexington was a good school, and it was only about eighty miles from Cincinnati, so my parents could see me play. Kentucky offered me a baseball scholarship. I had it all figured out: I would play for one year at Kentucky, get drafted, sign a contract, play pro ball, and make a fortune. Once again, I proceeded to elaborately create my own set of plans while God was quietly crafting his.

I headed off to University of Kentucky with an associate's degree in business and finance from Middle Georgia. I was one of only two players on the team to graduate. I'm very proud of that. It was a sure symbol of the good that came out of adversity. I was now more educated than my contemporaries and still in killer shape to play in the majors.

In Kentucky I met a girl named Donna. She was a track star from Canada. We dated my entire junior year. It felt good being monogamous again, familiar and right. We were a great match: two athletes with aspirations to take our abilities beyond the college level—the Canadian Olympic team for Donna and the major leagues for me. I thought she was the one (again). We were in love, and we'd support each other when the pros came knocking for us. While I had been wrong several times before, this time I knew for sure that my junior year at Kentucky would be my last in college, so I made the most of it while remaining committed to my relationship with Donna. I led the team in hits with an average of about .380 with thirteen home runs. When the season ended in 1985 I knew I would be drafted. Once again, I wasn't. My dreams of a career in pro ball were starting to fade.

The odds of an undrafted player making the major leagues are astronomically high. Teams have scouts covering the United States and other countries, too, so when

draft day comes, they have a good idea of which pros-
pects will fill their future needs. With each passing year,
I was competing against more and more talent that was
sometimes better, younger, and healthier. I was twenty-
two years old and not yet washed up. I knew there would
still be a possibility to be drafted after my senior year, but
the odds were slim.

My roommate in Lexington, Rusty Schuler, who was
our center fielder, lived in Hays, Kansas. He convinced
me to play summer baseball there for the Larks of the
National Baseball Congress (NBC). This was a league
comprised of college players hoping to be noticed by
the scouts. I could get away, have some fun, and try to
get over my disappointment at not being drafted again. I
had no other career plans; I still believed I had a chance
to play professional baseball and this collegiate league
would give me more exposure. I knew I was good enough.
I also knew that I could outwork and outhustle anybody.
All I needed was the opportunity.

Frank Leo, the Larks coach, told me that he didn't
understand why I hadn't been drafted. He told me to
work hard in Hays and said that there were lots of big-
league scouts watching our games. Frank really encouraged me. I spent a lot of time with Frank, his wife Barb,

and their two daughters, Lindsey and Gina. The two of us and another teammate helped Frank paint houses during the day to earn our keep. They took great care of me and became my second family. One night after dinner, Barb even permed my hair. They took pictures of me with my hair in curlers and used to tease me that after I made the major leagues they were going to show all my teammates. Frank took notice of the extra work I was putting in. I would stay after practice and work on running bases and getting a good jump when stealing second base. I had a good year with the Larks. I had a .416 batting average and thirteen home runs in 1985. They are still the fourth best in team history. My seventy-two hits put me in fifth position and my sixty-six RBIs were good enough for second position. I also had twenty-one doubles which are still the second most in team history. Other Hays players who have played in the major leagues after me were Lance Berkman and Albert Poulos.

One day, during the NBC tournament, Doug Melvin and Bill Livesey were in the stands watching us play. Melvin was a Yankee scout and later the general manager of the Milwaukee Brewers. Livesey was a Yankees' cross-checker. (When a scout reports to his team that they should take a look at a young player, the team sends the cross-checker as a follow-up.) I didn't even know I was being scouted. They told me, "Jim, we think you can hit. We don't know where you're going to play. We know you want to catch. We also know that you can play third and the outfield. But we're going to put you down as a hitter. Let *them* figure it out."

I had a very good NBC series. By the end of it, Livesey said that the Yankees were interested in signing me and sending me to spring training in 1986. There was also a scout from the Kansas City Royals who wanted to offer me a contract. We went back and forth a little. When I told my father of the teams' interest in me, he flew out to Wichita. That is one of the things I love best about my father. Whether I was having a crisis, or experiencing something very good and needed his support, he was always there. The Yankees offered me a signing bonus of $8,000, and they would also pay for me to finish college. Kansas City couldn't match the Yankees' offer, so we decided to go with New York. Dad's theory was just get your foot in the door. The rest would come if you worked hard and never gave up. A sum of $8,000 seemed like a lot of money for playing baseball. My father said, "You want the Yankees? Let's go!"

I called Keith Madison, my coach at Kentucky, and asked him, "If I come back to Kentucky, can I catch?" He said no. Although my foot was healed enough, he had Greg Stephens, a senior catcher who was already there, and he wanted me to stay at third base. I was later informed by one of the scouts that Coach Madison had said I didn't want to sign professionally and wanted to finish my senior year instead. When I heard this I was very upset as I had been crystal clear with Coach Madison about my desire to sign. The next day I signed a minor-league contract with the Yankees.

I enrolled for the fall semester at Kentucky. I thought that Madison would be happy that one of his former players had signed with the pros, but I was wrong. He was angry for two reasons: (1) Since the Yankees signed me so late, Madison didn't have time to recruit someone to replace me with a scholarship, and (2) he believed that I had planned this the whole time. I was ineligible to play because I was now a professional, although I could continue to work out with the team throwing batting practice. My former teammates were very excited for me. When Madison found out I was working out with them, he kicked me out. I didn't understand why he wouldn't want the other players to see that if they worked as hard as I had, they too could go on to a professional career. So I finished up the fall semester, leaving Kentucky with some disappointment at the way it had ended.

I headed to Fort Lauderdale in March 1986. I drove for sixteen hours, just imagining what the moment would be like when I put on my first professional uniform. *I was going to get paid to play baseball!* I knew it wouldn't be long before I'd see my first major-league pitch. This was just the first step.

I reported to the minor-league spring training site in

Fort Lauderdale, Florida, where I would be joining the rest of the minor league players. It wasn't the major leagues yet, but I was a professional ballplayer—and I was a Yankee. Bill Livesey, the scout who signed me, told the Yankees, "This guy's a hitter—find a place for him in the field." So, at the start of camp, my position was up in the air. I had to play third base and the outfield in college because my high school foot injury hadn't fully healed. When the minor-league coach asked me which position I played, I said, "Catcher first, but I can also play first base, third base, and outfield." Despite not having caught for a few years, I really wanted the chance to play behind the plate. I felt that catching was the quickest way to the big leagues.

3

Catching On

Catching is one of the fastest ways to get to the big leagues, since every team is constantly searching for catchers, the most physically demanding position. A few days into spring training, I discovered another.

One day, I was following Pete Rose's advice to keep my body balanced and stay loose by switch-hitting in the batting cage. Roy White, a former Yankee star outfielder and spring-training instructor, noticed and said, "Do you realize that there aren't any young switch-hitting catchers in the Yankees organization at this time? You look like you can hit. If you can switch-hit and bat .250, you're going to get an opportunity to play in the big leagues."

I had begun to work with Roy White every day to learn how to hit left-handed. When spring training was almost over, the Yankees felt I needed more work on learning how to switch-hit. They had a program in Sarasota from April through June called "extended spring training" where players went to work on their weaknesses until they were ready to be sent to another minor-league team. Those who needed to improve had to wait for the rookie season to start, which wasn't until after the June draft. So I reported to Sarasota when all the other players left for their seasons in the minors.

William "Buck" Showalter, who later managed the Yankees, was the coach in charge of extended spring training. He liked the idea of me becoming a switch-hitter. Showalter saw potential in me, so we trained and trained. I did pretty well. Of course, most of the pitchers I faced didn't have much besides fastballs. I hit off the batting tee for two or three hours a day. I took extra batting practice every day. Besides this, I was also relearning how to catch, something that had been my dream since Johnny Bench showed me how to catch when I was a little boy.

By May, Buck felt I was ready to go to the next level:

the Single A Fort Lauderdale Yankees in the Florida State League. My rise to the major leagues had begun! I really believed that I was on the fast track, and, that within two years, I would be putting on the New York Yankees pinstripes. I could hear Yankee Stadium public address announcer Bob Sheppard in my sleep: "Now batting for the Yankees, number 14, Jim Leyritz, number 14."

Johnny Hawkins (our team's version of Crash Davis, the catcher portrayed by Kevin Costner in the movie *Bull Durham*) was one of the catchers in Fort Lauderdale. Mitch Lyden was the righty-hitting catcher, the Big Prospect. The manager was Russell Earl "Bucky" Dent, whose famous home run in the 1978 American League playoff propelled the Yankees to victory in one of the most famous games in Yankee history.

I quickly learned that at this level, switch-hitting would be much more difficult. I was often swinging at pitches that hit me on my back leg. The pitchers were a little more established, throwing breaking balls and changing speeds. I was embarrassed. I couldn't adjust to pitches that moved all over the plate: sliders, curveballs, and so on. The young kids in extended spring training threw mostly fastballs, which were easier to hit. I was struggling horribly from the left side of the plate. To make matters worse, catching was also getting harder. Every time you move up in the minor leagues, the pitchers throw harder and have different movement on their pitches. I was starting to get frustrated.

Though catching was tough, I was so happy to be behind the plate that I didn't care about sore legs or bumps from being hit by occasional foul balls. This was what I wanted. But the switch-hitting wasn't going as well. I struggled for about a week to tell Bucky I didn't want to switch-hit any longer. I decided that learning how to switch-hit and relearning catching was too much to master all at once. I remembered Bill Livesey saying, "Jimmy, you're a hitter." So I decided to continue catching but give up switch-hitting. I felt I could hit right-handed full-time and could hit anybody. I went into Dent's office and told him I wanted to stop hitting left-handed. I just wanted to bat righty. Bucky told me if I abandoned switch-hitting, I was gone; that was the only reason I was there. I told him if I had to switch-hit to stay, then get rid of me. We had quite an argument. I stuck to my guns, and Dent shipped me out to Single A rookie ball in Oneonta, New York. Although this was a setback, I knew I would never make the major leagues by switch-hitting. Buck Showalter was the manager, and Hall of Famer Hoyt Wilhelm was the pitching coach. My teammates included future big leaguers Andy Stankiewicz, Turner Ward, John Ramos, Hal Morris, Kevin Maas, Steve Adkins, Oscar Azócar, Tim Layana, Ken Patterson, Steve Rosenberg, Rich Scheid, and Dean Wilkins.

The Oneonta Yankees played at Damaschke Field, the

only minor-league park in America that does not serve beer. I hit .363 batting just righty against both left- and right-handed pitchers. I knew I could do it. And just as I was finding my groove and getting the attention I wanted and deserved, wouldn't you know I tore some cartilage in my left knee and had my first surgery. Dr. Daniel Kannel, the Yankee team surgeon, performed the surgery in New York City. Here we went again, another bump in the road on my journey to the major leagues.

In 1987, I went to spring training again with the Yankees, who promoted me to the Fort Lauderdale Yankees in the Class A Florida State League. I hit .307 batting righty and won the Florida State League (South) batting title. Among my teammates (in addition to Azócar, Maas, Stankiewicz, and Ward) were Hensley "Bam Bam" Meulens and Bernie Williams, future big leaguers with the Yankees. I led the league in throwing out runners and in hitting, but I also led the league in passed balls. Pitchers in the Florida State League were significantly better than the pitchers I'd been used to, and it took me some time to get acclimated to their pitching.

My main problem was with passed balls, which are usually caused by lack of focus and the movement of the pitches. Behind the plate, I'd put down a sign for the pitcher and sometimes forget what it was because I was thinking about the out I had just made up at bat. I thought of myself as a hitter first and then a catcher. A good catcher, especially a big league catcher, has to be both a hitter *and* a position player. That's the nature of baseball. We don't have one team for offense and a different team for defense. I have to give our manager, Buck Showalter, a lot of credit. He worked hard with me, trying to help me separate my offense from my defense. He lived, breathed, ate, and slept Yankee baseball—by the book.

While I was making progress up the Yankee ladder, albeit slowly, all of the shuffling around and moving made it difficult for me to keep relationships. With my lifestyle, it was almost inevitable that if I were to meet that special someone, it would have to be on the road. While at the University of Florida in Gainesville, Chris Lambordozzi, Scott Lusader, and I decided that in the off-season, we would stay at Chi Phi, one of the fraternity houses on campus, and work out together. This is where I met my first wife, Andi. She was a junior and very beautiful. I was struck by her instantly. We started dating that off-season, and I continued to stay in touch with her as the new season began.

I started the 1988 season with Albany-Colonie, the Yankees' AA team in the Eastern League. This was a step up from the Fort Lauderdale Yankees. The pitchers had more control and the batters had a little more power and better batting eyes. The players were also more experienced on the bases—tougher for the catchers to throw out. Tommy Jones was the manager, later succeeded by Carl "Stump" Merrill, who went on to manage the Yankees in 1990 and 1991. In Albany-Colonie, I played with Maas, Stankiewicz, and Meulens again.

During the first game of the 1988 season, I was hit in the face by a pitch. I turned into the ball, instead of away. I was knocked out and my lip was split. When I eventually got up, I instinctively ran to first base. My teeth were still caught in my gum. I'm told that the trainer shouted: "Stop! Stop! Stop!" but I don't remember any of this. The next thing I knew, I was on the training table. Somebody was looking at me, saying that I had not broken any teeth. I was taken to the hospital and examined for a concussion. I had a number of stitches in my lip, but two days later, I was back in the lineup. Manager Tommy Jones wanted me to take more time off, but I told him that if I didn't get back up at the plate, I'd be afraid to face live pitching. I didn't want that. I couldn't catch because the catcher's mask wouldn't fit over my swollen face.

My first time back at the plate, I hit a double. Wham! I was back. Even if my lips looked like they belonged on a platypus, I had shown the Yankees that I could dust myself off and take care of business. My call up to the big leagues was sure to be on its way. But two weeks later, I tore a ligament in my left ankle, and I was out for four weeks.

That was some bumpy road. I did not have surgery, but I was on crutches for a week, and then in a walking cast for three more weeks. Those thirty days seemed endless. I was frustrated as all hell. No matter how hard I tried, I couldn't catch a break. Just when I seemed to push that boulder to the top of the mountain, it came rolling back down on me and continued to steamroll me for good measure. What did it take for me to stay healthy, to show my stuff, and get the hell out of the minors?

Then, a few weeks after the walking cast came off, I broke a finger on my throwing hand. It was a bad couple of months. Sitting on the bench became a liability for me, as my psyche began to suffer and my belief in hard work and persistence became jaded. I thought to myself that I should just quit.

I prayed for guidance and asked God, *Is this the path I'm supposed to be on?* I was going to call my dad and inform him that I was thinking of quitting. He'd been there through it all with me, and I never made any decisions without consulting him: junior college, Hays, Kansas, the Yankees. My father told me to stick it out, that the *real* world would always be there and to keep playing until they told me to go home. Then I spoke with one of my best friends, Joe Datin. Joe had just been released by the Los Angeles Dodgers. He was home in Cincinnati, working at a "regular" job. He told me not to quit until they tore the uniform off me. I'd have plenty of time for the real world *after* my baseball career. Joe and my father said virtually the same thing to me and I felt that this was God giving me my answer. I decided *not* to quit.

I used the time off to strengthen my mind and my will. I used it to my advantage, to regroup instead of throwing myself a pity party. It worked. When I came back, hitting coach Deron Johnson trained me to become a power hitter. His technique was to teach me to bat with my hands lower on the bat. I stayed with it. Changing my batting stance was hard for me, and my batting average dropped to .240.

We won the Eastern League championship in 1988. Although there is no bonus money for minor leaguers when they win the league championship, I did get a commemorative ring. I was lucky enough to win four minor-league championships: the Florida State League in 1987, two AA Albany-Colonie (Eastern League) in 1988 and 1989, and the International League championship with AAA Columbus in 1991.

In 1989, I started my first spring training with the big-league club. The Yankees were trying to teach me how to play second base that spring. I had very good spring training—so good, in fact, that I thought I'd earned a promotion to the Columbus Clippers, the Yankees' AAA team in the International League, the highest level in the minors and just a phone call away from the majors. But I was sent back to the Albany-Colonie Yankees at AA. What I took as a demotion (even though I was just sent back to where I'd been in Albany) just made me more determined to play so well that the Yankees would have to promote me.

I lived in the college dormitory at SUNY-Albany with Dave Eiland, Bobby Green, and John Ramos. "Bam Bam" Meulens and Mike Blowers were promoted to Columbus. I went back to Albany to play for the new manager Buck Showalter.

The Albany-Colonie team did very well. We went 70 and 30 at one point and finished 92–48. One of our pitchers, Rodney Imes, was 17–6, but even *that* wasn't good enough to earn him a promotion. At that time, the Yankees wanted their pitchers to pitch 140 innings at each level before they would even consider promoting them to the majors. I had another good year (.315 with ten home runs) and we were in the play-offs again.

Over that year, Andi and I became very close—so much so that we talked of moving in together in Albany when she graduated. One night I invited her to come up to Albany for a few days. During one of the games that week, I had set up a marriage proposal on the scoreboard. The club was great and ran the message in the middle of game. Andi said yes, and on November 11, 1989, we got married at the First Baptist Church in Fort Lauderdale. We were together for a year during my minor-league career and a year in the majors, but we started having problems after that.

When 1990 rolled around, I went to spring training at the major-league camp in Fort Lauderdale. I was still catching, but I was also playing second and third base. I had played all over at AA. John Ramos and I switched off from catching and the outfield. I had another very good spring, and up until the very last day of spring training, I thought I was going to make the big club. I had hit my stride for sure, and had become the utility player that adds value to the team. I was ready, willing, and able to do anything. In fact, in addition to my catcher's mitts (I carried two), I also carried two first baseman's mitt, a third baseman's glove, a second baseman's glove (which is slightly smaller than a third baseman's glove, to make it easier to get the ball out quickly for a double play), and a larger outfielder's glove. I still have my first Mizuno third baseman's glove with my name on it. Behind the plate, I used an All-Star brand mitt. I found that although the Rawlings mitts lasted longer, the All-Star mitts were much easier to break in.

Third baseman Hensley "Bam-Bam" Meulens had not turned out to be the player the Yankees thought he would be. In eight games, he had twenty-eight at bats, hit .179 with just one RBI, and four errors at third base. General manager George Bradley told me that the Yankees wanted me to play third base every day—at Columbus!

Up to this time, I had spent my entire childhood and

adult sports career imagining, wishing, and planning for the big time. And once I made it to Columbus, it was even better than in my wildest dreams. I think having so many close calls is what made this moment sweeter. Even after all the adversity and almost quitting, I still saw going to Columbus as an attainable goal. I knew that once I was there, I would give them what they wanted, and the majors would be just a phone call away. The road to the major leagues so far had been paved with coal, but I swear that if it weren't for those years of agony, of trying and trying and still not reaching my ultimate goal, I wouldn't have been ready to kick butt in Columbus.

God had a plan and it was to test me—injury after injury, argument after argument, rejection after rejection. What didn't kill me made me stronger, and if I had to do it all over again, I wouldn't change a thing. I know it's a cliché, but nothing worth achieving is achieved easily. But I only know that *now*, after having so much time to reflect on the brilliance of it all.

The Clippers' managers in 1990 were Rick Down (later the Yankees' hitting coach) and Stump Merrill. In Columbus, I was on a team that was comprised of mostly future major leaguers: Oscar Azócar, Andy Stankiewicz, Kevin Maas, Hensley Meulens, Wade Taylor, Britt Burns, Mike Blowers, Bob Brower, Rick Cerone, Bob Davidson, Ron Davis, Dave Eiland (later the Yankees' pitching coach), Jimmy Jones, Lance McCullers, Alan Mills,

Kevin Mmahat, Rich Monteleone, Clay Parker, Hipólito Peña, Jeff Datz, Mike Smith, Willie Smith, Van Snider, Brian Dorsett, John Fishel, John Habyan, Mitch Lyden, Carlos Rodríguez, Deion Sanders, Dave Sax, Jim Walewander, and Mark Wasinger.

For a twenty-six-year-old player who had fought his way up to Columbus, I had no right to be as cocky as I was. I didn't want to believe it, but part of the reason I was still at AAA was the run-in I had had with Bucky Dent in Single A years earlier. If he hadn't been the manager of the Yankees, I knew I would have made the big league club out of camp. But after forty-nine games, Dent—with a dismal 18–31 record—was fired as the Yankee manager and replaced by Stump Merrill. I don't believe it was coincidence that three days later, I was called up to the big leagues.

I remember the night very well. The Clippers were in Toledo to play the Mud Hens in a battle between Ohio's two AAA teams. I thought that manager Rick Down was calling me into his office to discuss my hitting—or lack thereof. I had gone 0–6 in a doubleheader. Alan Mills, a right-handed pitcher, walked into Down's office with me. It was one o'clock in the morning, so I knew something was up. Down told us that we were both going to the big leagues—the fulfillment of my lifelong dream. I called my parents and my wife Andi to share the incredible news. My parents were half asleep, but when I told them the good news, they both broke down and cried. Tears of happiness, of course. I let them know that I wouldn't play the first day but probably the second or third day. They made reservations to fly to Baltimore the next day. Andi wanted to be there too but she had to stay in Columbus to pack up our apartment. The team would only be in Baltimore for three days and after that we would be heading back to Yankee Stadium. She would join me in New York for my Yankee Stadium debut. The minor league days were over and I was elated. Little did we realize just how much our lives were going to change.

Mills and I flew from Toledo to Baltimore together. We were walking on air! We got to our hotel in Baltimore at about 3:30 in the afternoon. We dropped our bags at the hotel and arrived at Memorial Stadium just as batting practice was ending. We didn't even get to warm up. I already knew some of the players on the Yankees, like Steve Saxe and Dave LaPoint, because we had played together earlier in spring training. I knew most of the rest of the team by reputation; I had been following them in the sports pages. The clubhouse guy gave me a pair of Yankee pants: ironically, the name sewn inside the pants was *Bucky Dent*.

4

They Don't Call It Memorial Stadium for Nothing!

I *finally made it,* I thought as I suited up for my first big-
league game at Baltimore's Memorial Stadium. Even
though I laced my spikes with the knowledge that I'd be
watching the game against the Orioles from the dugout,
I didn't care. I had still made it—I had the pinstripes to
prove it. I considered how my parents were feeling, how

proud they were of me, and that all of my hard work finally paid off. And theirs as well: those sacrifices they made were worth it in the end, when I was called by Steinbrenner to be a part of the world's most recognizable sports franchise— the New York Yankees.

I sat at the end of the dugout staying out of the way and taking it all in. I was finally watching a game from a big-league dugout with a stadium that could hold 50,000 cheering fans. The ballpark in Columbus only seated about 17,000. What a thrill! As I sat there, all I could do was think back to all the sacrifices and hard work that got me there. But I could still hear my dads voice bellowing, "Don't ever be satisfied with just being there!" Around the fifth inning, with the Orioles ahead 3–2, bench coach Buck Showalter walked over and said to me, "Be ready to hit in the late innings. Stump likes to throw you right into the fire." With a twinge in my gut, I got up and went into the clubhouse to stretch and get loose, as loose as one can get right before he is about to get his first major-league at bat.

I watched the game on the television in the clubhouse. In the eighth inning, I saw Gregg Olson warming up in the Orioles' bullpen. By that time in the season, Olson was one of the game's best closers. He had a nasty curveball and was a perfect 13–13 in save opportunities. As I saw him warming up, I figured my pinch-hitting chances were gone.

The Orioles were ahead 4–3. In the top of the ninth,

Yankees' third baseman Randy Velarde grounded out on one of Olson's killer curveballs, and left fielder "Neon" Deion Sanders (who was elected to the Pro Football Hall of Fame in 2011) struck out. The next batter, second baseman Steve Sax, singled to right. Due up with two outs was light-hitting shortstop Wayne Tolleson, but Stump decided shortly beforehand that I'd pinch-hit for him. Showalter gave me the signal, and that was that: with just the command of Showalter's nod, I walked up to the plate for my first at bat. It's a feeling that you never forget. I think I probably felt much like a young bride might feel walking down the aisle, recalling all the days that led up to this one.

As I approached the plate, I got chills of excitement hearing my name announced by the Orioles' public-address announcer. I thought about all the long days of working extra late, fitful arguments with coaches and managers, searching for mentors, being passed over, yo-yo promotions and demotions, scouts, injuries, and of almost quitting. Now I was a Yankee, at the plate, ready to make my mark—at last. The ballpark was not quite sold out. But 44,000 pairs of eyes were on me.

Olson's first pitch was a fifty-eight-foot curveball in the dirt that I couldn't resist swinging at. I was overanxious. My desire to have my bat make contact with the first pitch overwhelmed my judgment. Mickey Tettleton, the Oriole's catcher, blocked it, but Steve Sax was able to steal second base. The next pitch was another curveball, and again I swung and missed. Now I was down 0–2. I thought, *Okay, just foul something off to save face.* The next pitch was a fastball up and away. I didn't swing. Ball one. I was able to exhale and relax a little. Then Olson went back to the curveball, but this time I hit a line drive foul ball down the first base line that almost hit Yankees' first base coach Mike Ferraro. With that, I gained a little confidence. *You can hit this guy.*

The next pitch was another curveball. This time though, he hung it out over the plate, and I hit it for a single through the hole at short, which sent Sax home with the game-tying run. I had my first major-league hit and my first RBI just like that, in my first at bat! Olson had his first blown save of the season. What a memory. They don't call it Memorial Stadium for nothing!

Randy Milligan was the Orioles' first baseman. He called for the ball and then threw it into the Yankees' dugout saying, "Good job, kid. Way to battle." I looked up and quietly thanked God for giving me this moment. The ball was my souvenir—a customary courtesy for a rookie's first hit. I gave the ball to my father, who still has it.

After Don Mattingly grounded out to short for the third out, I went into the dugout, got my glove, and went out to play third base. (Velarde had moved from third to shortstop.) I was pumped. I had just had the game-tying hit. The Orioles loaded the bases. I was playing in front of the bag for a play at the plate. A ground ball came my way and I made a dive for it, stopped it in its tracks, and made the play to home with the intent of cutting off runner Milligan, who was racing there. Instead, I short-hopped to catcher Matt Nokes, who couldn't handle the throw. Milligan scored from third and the game was over: E6. A more experienced third baseman would have stepped on third and thrown to first for the double play, but I was green and overambitious and got the error as a result. We lost 5–4 on the error.

Nevertheless, my first day in the big leagues was bittersweet. Getting my first hit and RBI was a huge thrill, but my first error had cost us the game. I tried not to let it get to me. I didn't want it to outshine the significance of the day. The dreams and hopes of my younger days were finally being fulfilled.

The next day, with my parents in the stands, I replaced Jesse Barfield, the regular right fielder, in the ninth inning. In my one at bat, I struck out in the ninth to end the game. On June 10, I made my first start—at third base. I singled, doubled, scored a run, struck out looking, and made an error. My mom and dad waited for me after the game and said good-bye as I boarded the team bus. They both gave me a hug and told me how proud they were.

My Yankee Stadium debut came on June 13, 1990. Andi had finally joined me, and we stayed at a hotel in the city our first night. The city was huge and somewhat overwhelming. But I was taking it all in. My agent David Lihn came over and showed me how to take the subway train to the Stadium. I remember riding the train and Andi looking a little scared. We had heard of all the horror stories about New York subways. Then the stop I had been waiting for (River Avenue and 161st Street) was announced over the intercom. Andi and I got out and just looked around. We were here: Yankee Stadium. Wow. A little different from the minor-league ballparks we were used to seeing. As I walked to the entrance of the Stadium, the butterflies began. I started thinking about where I was and the pressures that go with playing for the Yankees in front of their New York fans. Andi asked me how I felt as we entered the tunnel that led to the field. I told her I was excited and ready for this new chapter.

I knew the New York fans were a very demanding crowd in their expectations for their beloved team, a team that at this time was in last place and not playing very well. On top of that, this series was against their biggest rival—the Boston Red Sox—so we would be playing in a packed house. I went into the locker room and could truly feel the pride guys always talk about when they are blessed to wear the pinstripes. Once I had the uniform on, I remember thinking to myself, *You truly have arrived.* I wasn't in the starting linup that night. I wasn't expecting to make my debut, but in the bottom of the eighth inning, it happened. With the Yankees trailing 2–1, I pinch-hit for shortstop Alvaro Espinoza against Roger Clemens, one of the greatest pitchers of all time. I stood on the on-deck circle and tried to imagine what it would feel like when I finally heard Bob Sheppard, the legendary Yankee PA announcer, give me my official introduction to the Yankee home fans. As I approached the plate, the stadium seemed almost silent as his booming voice announced, "Now batting number 12, Jim Leyritz, number 12."

I didn't get nervous until I stepped into the batter's box. I looked up and saw Roger Clemens on the mound. I saw my name on the scoreboard and I tried to focus. Before I knew it, he was in his windup, ready to throw me a fastball. Ball one. Then a second fastball. Strike one. His third pitch was a slider, and I was right on it. I singled to right field and began running down first base for my first Yankee Stadium hit. As I came back to shake first-base coach Mike Ferrero's hand, our first base coach, I was lifted for a pinch runner, the speedy Claudell Washington. I went back into the dugout and again thanked the good Lord for this incredible moment. This would be just the beginning of many memories and lessons that I would experience on this historic field.

That first game at Memorial Stadium taught me a lot— about the game, about my capabilities, about resiliency.

Even though I had swung weakly at the first pitch—a pitch in the dirt!—I had regained control of myself and got a hit. In my first at bat against Roger Clemens, I got another hit.

Surprisingly, what I needed to learn most, but was learning more slowly, was the dynamic of the team, specifically, what it's like to be the new guy, the rookie. The first flight that I took with the team was a flight from Baltimore back to New York. I'd never been on a private jet before and the guys piled onto the plane casually, as I scanned the cabin to figure out where I should sit. There weren't necessarily assigned seats, but for the most part the seating arrangements went something like this: born-again Christians sat at the front, beer drinkers sat in the back, and cardplayers sat in the middle. I was a cardplayer, so I sat in the middle section. After losing two hands, I decided that I wanted to have a beer. So I got up and moved to the back of the plane.

Dave Righetti, one of the Yankees' veteran lefty pitchers, noticed me passing through and said, "Rook, what do you think you're doing?" I answered, "I'm getting a beer. I'm thirsty." He looked at me as if I was trespassing. So I added, "Is there a problem with that?" He answered me with a tone that seemed like he was challenging me. I repeated, "I'm grabbing a beer, just like you're doing." He told me there was a certain protocol I had to adhere to, and that was to ask permission to come to the back of the plane. I looked at him and said, "Hey man, I'm just one of twenty-five guys on this team, you ain't no different than me." I was not backing down. But before the whole situation could escalate, pitcher Dave LaPoint and second baseman Steve Sax—who didn't drink but sat with the beer drinkers to crack jokes—helped diffuse the situation. LaPoint stepped in and said to me, "Come here." He explained to me the protocols of rookie behavior on the team plane. Ultimately, the message was that while I was technically a member of the team, I had to earn my right to sit with the veterans. As a rookie, I was supposed to be subordinate and understand that I wasn't equal to the older guys on the team. Therefore, my roaming up the aisle, acting entitled to a beer, didn't jibe with the acceptable rookie behavior. This was a part of the game that I never truly believed in. After all, this was not a winning team, and at this point I felt the reason I was brought up was to help them win. I learned as the years went on that I was right. The teams who had twenty-five guys who were all treated equally and operated as more of a family were usually the winning teams. This would not be last time I challenged what was considered to be policy or the company line.

I hit my first big-league home run off Mélido Pérez of the Chicago White Sox on June 30, 1990, at Comisky Park. Mélido's brother Pascual pitched for us. As a catcher, of course, I spent virtually the entire game watching pitchers. While on the bench, I'd try to study the other team's pitchers. By the second inning, the players on the bench figured out that he was tipping his pitches, unintentionally using his body to give a sign as to which pitch he was about to throw: with his finger out of his glove, Mélido shook his finger for a fastball but not for a slider. He also had a good split-fingered fastball, but we thought if we could eliminate one out of three, that would help us a lot. I saw his finger, knew he was throwing a slider, adjusted my swing, and hit his first pitch for a two-run home run. Ken Patterson, with whom I had played in the minors, relieved Pérez in the ninth and I homered off him, too.

The next day, Stump Merrill put me back in the lineup to face Greg Hibbard of the White Sox. Instead of third base, Stump asked me to play left field, my first game in the outfield since AA in 1989. Mike Blowers played third.

While there are no degrees of errors, not all errors are created equal. I know this firsthand and will never forget the day I made the error to end all errors: July 1, 1990. The Andy Hawkins game. In the first play of the game, Lance Johnson of the Chicago White Sox hit a ball to left field. I ran back to the fence, but the wind blew the ball in. I made a sliding catch almost back on the infield. It was a nice play, and I was pumped. By the eighth inning, Yankee pitcher Andy Hawkins, a big right-hander from Waco, Texas, still hadn't given up a hit. The score was tied at 0. Then Robin Ventura hit a medium line drive to me. I thought the wind would hold it up because it had blown Lance Johnson's ball back earlier. But this ball wasn't hit high enough for the wind to hold it up. I had misjudged it. I tried to backpedal and catch it anyway. I barely got to the ball and was able to do a pirouette under the ball and it hit my glove. But then I dropped it for a three-run error. Hawkins still had a no-hitter, though, because of the three runs were scored on my error. We were now losing 3–0.

The next hitter, Iván Calderón, hit a routine fly ball to Jesse Barfield in right field that should have been the third out. But the wind and the sun were so bad that Jesse did the same thing. He got to the ball, but it hit off his glove for the third error that inning. Now the White Sox led 4–0. Hawkins got the next hitter out and the inning was over, the no-hitter still intact. We didn't score in the ninth. A double play ended the game. We lost 4–0.

The New York media was all over me: How did I feel? What did it feel like to lose a no-hitter? How was I going to deal with this? After the game, I told reporters, "Ventura hit it right at me. I made the wrong move to the wrong side, and the wind didn't hold it up. I didn't think I could catch up to it. When I did, it hit the top of my glove. You get down on yourself because you hate to lose a no-hitter on something like that, but that's baseball. Tomorrow is another day."

I found out then just how brutal the New York media was going to be. The next day the papers reported that I was "cavalier" in my attitude about dropping the fly ball. They made it sound as if I didn't feel bad for Hawkins. Thank God, Andy knew better. I had apologized to him profusely before the reporters had come into the locker room. All my teammates had also come up to me and said, "Keep your head up, kid—that was tough sun and wind out there today." I was hitting well and playing hard. I was earning my teammates' respect. The support still didn't help me feel any better about losing, but I was glad they thought enough of me to take the initiative to come over and try to make me feel better about it.

Hawkins threw eight innings of no-hit ball, but his effort was diminished by three Yankee errors in one inning, four unearned runs, and no run support. He was the hard-luck loser. But the wound was reopened a year later, when the no-hitter status was ripped away from him by a change in rules by the office of the baseball commissioner. Major League Baseball revised its definition of a no-hitter, declaring that to be an "official" no-hitter, a starting pitcher had to pitch nine innings and win. Hawkins's no-hitter was wiped out.

The Andy Hawkins game taught me an important lesson about big-league baseball and about the media: both
were fickle. The night before I had been the hero, hitting
my first two major-league home runs and helping us win.
The next day I was the goat. I learned that in baseball,
every day brings an opportunity for a new beginning, and
in New York you were only as good as your last at bat
or play. It reminded me of what my dad had always told
me when I was younger. The fans would forgive you if
you redeemed yourself, but they'd never forget. New York
City is one tough city to succeed in if you don't have a
backbone. While many guys over the years couldn't handle the pressures of playing in New York, I loved every
minute of it.

The summer came and went, and our record was dismal. The Yanks were on their way to finish last in the
American League East. I spent the months playing different positions. So, as promised, my bat did talk. I started
out hitting and hitting. But, most of all, the Yankees
liked the enthusiasm that I brought to the ballpark every
day. Leaving it all on the field was the cliché that was
used to describe how people felt I played the game. On
September 19, 1990, in the sixth inning with one man on
base, I hit a home run off Blue Jays pitcher Jim Acker in

Toronto—the longest home run I ever hit. The Skydome (now the Rogers Centre) used to have a clock in the third deck. I hit it.

I was a young player trying to establish myself. During the winter of 1990 I had made myself available for appearances to promote the Yankees. I participated in every Yankee caravan, an off-season ritual in which players visit schools, hospitals, and clinics, making a difference in the community and getting people interested in buying tickets for the upcoming season. I was so proud to be a part of the team. I wanted to do everything right and show the powers that be that I was a team player on and off the field.

In the early 1990s, the Yankees, under managers Bucky Dent and Stump Merrill, were terrible. They finished 67–95, dead last in the American League East. The team was stocked with many aging veterans like catcher Rick Cerone and pitcher Dave Righetti. I was one of the first young players to be with the Yankees in a long time. Outfielder Roberto Kelly, first baseman Kevin Mass, pitcher Alan Mills, and I were labeled "the Young Guns" by the press.

In 1991, the Yankees were going in a new direction. While Mr. Steinbrenner had been out on suspension for violating baseball policy (1990–1992), Gene "Stick" Michael had taken over as GM and began building the big-league club with the younger players. At the start of the 1991 season, they made a video of all of us and cut in scenes from the movie *Young Guns* and handed posters out at games. This was the new regime. It put a lot of pressure on us to back up all the hype.

At the time, a lot of minor-league players felt they would never get a chance to play for the Yankees, because the team was always signing free agents. The attitude was, play great in the minors for the Yankees and someone else would trade for you and you would be in the big leagues right away. Now with the Young Guns, these minor leaguers saw hope. Next came outfielder Oscar Azócar, then future star centerfielder Bernie Williams.

Fortunately, Kevin Maas and I got off to great starts the previous year and convinced Michael to continue giving young players in the team's farm system an opportunity to play for the Yankees. Maas came up late at age twenty-five on June 29, 1990, and hit ten home runs in his first seventy-two at bats, the most homers ever in the fewest at bats at the start of a career. The Yankees were grooming Kevin to succeed Don Mattingly, who was twenty-nine in 1990. If either of us had fallen on our faces, other young players in the Yankees' system might not have been given a chance.

The Yankees began to change their losing ways. Had Steinbrenner been back, he most likely would have preferred to sign established free agents—big stars like slugging first baseman Cecil Fielder, pitcher Luis Tiant, and future Hall of Famers Reggie Jackson and Catfish Hunter—rather than give young players from within the Yankee system a chance. And although he was still out on suspension, he loved being in the headlines. He fumed whenever the back pages of the two New York tabloids, the *Daily News* and the *New York Post*, had stories about or photos of the Mets. To "The Boss," a big Yankee signing was big news, sure to get the Yankees' picture in the paper, frequently on the back page. Promoting a player, no matter how good, from the Yankees' minor leagues to the Yankees was not something that would make the front or back page of the *News* or the *Post*. Calling us the Young Guns gave us some headlines and made good copy, not only for the beat reporters who covered the Yankees every day, but also for the sports columnists who wrote about not just who won but their opinions too: why something happened, who benefited, who was in the manager's doghouse, and who was rumored to be taking whose roster spot.

I think Michael liked me and appreciated my attitude. I told reporters, "I'm here to play. I'm here to make a difference." I was the type of guy he encouraged: hardworking, loyal, and ambitious, and I made big plays right out of the gate. The bigger the situation, the better I responded. I embraced those pressure situations that most players feared. Maybe I was cocky or confident, or maybe I was just too young to know any better. That's why Stick gave some other young kids the opportunity to play at the major-league level. Most of those players he gave a shot to did something outstanding right away, which validated Steinbrenner's faith in us and in Stick's decision to rebuild the Yankees from within.

When we opened the 1991 season in Detroit, I was the Yankees' Opening Day catcher. Tim Leary was our starting pitcher. My parents were at the game. Being named as an Opening Day starter at any position is an honor; it's a sign of respect. You've made it. You've arrived. You've succeeded. You're a vital part of the team. Or so I thought. For some reason known only to God, I didn't catch much after that. Instead, they played catchers Matt Nokes and Bob Geren, giving them more playing time and more visibility. Naturally, I was very upset that I wasn't playing. *Am I ever going to play regularly?* I wondered. *Hey, I caught on Opening Day!* I never said anything bad about Nokes or Geren, but I was pretty mad, especially because they weren't producing more than I was. I never thought I was better than them, but still, I thought I should at least be playing, too.

When I did play, I was put in late in the game in no-win situations: coming off the bench to face Dennis Eckersley, or Jeff Reardon, or some other team's ace reliever. I started the season 4 for 44, and was completely frustrated with the front office. We were on the road, and I couldn't speak to Stick personally, so I went into manager Stump

Merrill's office and asked why I wasn't starting. He told me he couldn't give me the answers that I wanted and that I would have to be patient. As I walked out of his office, Joel Sherman from the *New York Post* saw that I was visibly angry. He came by my locker and asked me what was wrong. I knew I shouldn't comment to the media before speaking with Stick but I was frustrated. I told Joel that I was sick and tired of waiting around (it was already the end of May) and said that I was going to tell the Yankees to "Play me or trade me." We were not a winning ball club, and I wanted to play more and help the team win. Joel's article came out the next day, and the front office was furious. They did not like players negotiating or complaining through the media.

When I got back to New York, I immediately went to see general manager Gene Michael. I thought I had earned some team credibility, and I felt slighted and misled by being told I had earned a starting role out of spring training. Again, I was questioning the Yankee's decisions and wanted to be in control. Instead of trusting God's plan, I marched into Stick's office and demanded answers. When I finished talking, he said that the Yankees were going to send me back to AAA Columbus. I erupted and pushed his desk in anger. "Screw you!" I yelled. "I'm not going anywhere with this organization. Get rid of me!" And then I stormed out.

I immediately turned to my agent and said, "You handle this. I'm done. I'm out of here." I went down to the clubhouse to get my things and stood by my locker. I told the reporters that I was not going to Columbus. It was crap. I said that the Yankees had lied to me and that I wanted a chance to play. I also called my father and told him what I'd done.

My father told me to shut my mouth and to get my ass to Columbus. He told me to let my *bat* do the talking. My dad told me that he agreed with me 100 percent but said, "What are you going to do? You've been in this situation before. You know that you can play in the majors but that you have to toe the company line. So shut your mouth and go to Columbus. And play well there."

The Yankees had assured me that once I got my stroke back in Columbus, I'd be back with them. I didn't really know how much to believe them, especially after the way I'd behaved in Gene Michael's office. But I sucked it up and made the drive to Columbus to join the Clippers. Once inserted as the Clippers' everyday catcher, I got off to a fast start, hitting four home runs in the first week. I called up the Yankees' front office and asked, "When am I coming back up?"

By that time, I'd fired my agent. I felt he was partly responsible for me being sent down because he did not speak up for me. Michael told me that I needed some more time at AAA. I knew this was bull. I knew that the

Yankees were playing games with me. When Don Mattingly got hurt, I was hitting .280 with eight home runs
for the Clippers, and I had been down there for six weeks.

The player the Yankees called up next was Torey
Lovullo, who, at the time, was hitting about .201. Lovullo
hit .224 with fifteen home runs during his eight-year big-
league career. That was a slap in the face for me. The
other players on the Clippers knew what was going on—
they got it and so did I. The Yankees were punishing me
for the comments I had made to the press.

The day Lovullo was called up, I told manager Rick
Down, "My head's not in the game. I'm not playing
today." He said, "Jimmy, if you do that, I have to call
Stick and let him know that you're in the lineup and you
don't want to play." I told him that I would be on the
bench, available if the team needed me to pinch-hit. I
didn't want to start.

During infield practice, Down came onto the field and
told me that he had spoken to Michael, who told him that
I was suspended if I wasn't going to play; I had to get
off the field. I said "fine," and left the field. In the clubhouse, I called my mother at her office at Midwest Invest-
ments, where she worked as an investment banker, and
told her what had happened. Her job put her in a position to know some good agents. I asked her to call Tom
Reich for me. Reich was one of the most respected agents
in the game. She knew him because she invested players'

money, like former Pittsburgh Pirates star Dave Parker, and some other players Tom represented. "Tell him that I need representation. I can't handle this situation myself." My mother called Reich.

I give Reich a lot of credit. After all, at the time I was a suspended rookie. But he called me and told me to stay around the ballpark. Let the scouts see me, and let them know what was going on, that all I wanted was more playing time and that the suspension was B.S.

The next night when I returned to my hotel room, I found a lock on the door. The Yankees had refused to continue to pay for it because I was suspended. The hotel manager told me that I could not enter the room until I gave him my credit card. I contacted Clippers' general manager Ken Schnacke and told him all the things I had done for the team. I said that I had been the most cordial player, doing all the events and meeting people in Columbus, even though I did not want to be down there. I told him that I thought this move was classless. When I called Tom Reich to tell him what had happened, he tried to calm me down. He told me to stay at the hotel. I think I spent four days in Pawtucket, Rhode Island, where the Clippers had been to play the Red Sox AAA team. Finally, after my five-day suspension, and Tom doing a lot of talking with the Yankees, Tom called to tell me to get my stuff and return to Columbus. He told me to just play hard and finish the season. We'd work on next year.

I was recalled to the Yankees again in September. My Yankee teammates all asked, "Dude, how did you ever get back here?" They all knew what had happened in Michael's office and down in AAA. To this day, I don't know why I was called back up. Clearly, God had a plan for me but I began to have serious reservations about playing for the Yankees. *Why would I want to be part of an organization that wasn't winning, that treated me the way they did, and didn't seem like they wanted me?* So even though I was not where I wanted to be, I knew I had to perform so other teams would want me. There were twenty six other teams I could go play for. Between pinch-hitting duties and playing third base and second base sporadically, I finished September hitting .310.

5

Change Up

After a dismal 1991, the Yankees desperately needed a strong 1992. Buck Showalter was named manager, and despite all of my problems with the front office, he wanted to bring me back for the 1992 season. Buck had been my manager in the minor leagues for three years and felt he could settle me down. I also felt more comfortable returning with him being there. I trusted Buck and felt he

would be straightforward with me. The strategy of building the team from within was working, and Buck and Stick
continued to bring in more young players. Mr. Steinbrenner
was no longer suspended and would be around the team
again. My agent, Tom Reich, and Mr. Steinbrenner were
very close and Tom spoke to George about me. Steinbrenner told Tom even though he didn't agree with everything I had done the previous year, he loved the way I stood
up and believed in myself. I had a great spring training,
and as we broke camp I knew this year would be pivotal
for me to establish a good relationship with management.
Early 1992 was the start of many changes.

The Yankees ended the 1992 season in fourth place, the
best finish we had since I had joined the team in 1990.
Although I still had not played as much as I liked, I
enjoyed playing for a team that was beginning to win. I
finished the season with only 144 at bats, but I had hit
seven home runs and drove in 26 runs. I also avoided any
run-ins with management, thanks to Buck's open line of
communication throughout the year. Before we left at the
end of the season, my agent Tom went to speak to Mr.
Steinbrenner. We wanted to see where we stood for the
1993 season. George complimented me for my positive
attitude throughout the year and assured Tom that next
year would be even better. Even the New York tabloids,
which had labeled me "selfish" in the past, were now
reporting what a team player I was.

I couldn't wait for the 1993 spring training to begin. We reported in February, and when we broke camp at the end of March, everything was falling into place. I played several different positions and Buck told me this would be my year to get the at bats I had complained about for so long. As Andi and I were packing to go back to New York, she created yet another bump in the road. She decided that she did not want to accompany me in New York for the season. She wanted to stay home in Florida and began working again, only visiting me in New York on occasional weekends. She was a talented animation artist and wanted to pursue a career of her own. I wasn't going to argue with her. I had made it to New York and was now a part of the most successful organization in all of sports. The fans and the city embraced me wholeheartedly, and I thought my career couldn't get any better. Everywhere I went, people recognized me and came up for autographs. Andi didn't like how public our relationship had become and had always wanted a quieter life; I think New York scared her a bit. I was too blind to see it at the time because I was so wrapped up in finally making it. I was going to soak in every thrilling opportunity: Ranger games, Knicks games, and the wild nightlife in the city that never sleeps. Unfortunately, the fact that we had completely different needs began to take a heavy toll on our relationship. We tried to make it work, but our weekends together became increasingly sparse and we spent more and more time apart.

Things started to deteriorate quickly. I took her absences to mean she wasn't supporting me and I was upset that she wasn't embracing this new life that I had sacrificed so much for. I began going out with the only other teammate who lived in New York City, Mel Hall. Mel was a veteran player who was making a lot of money and liked to live large. We spent many nights carousing the city, and I started living the life that my parents and God had kept me protected from for so long. I got caught up in it. I had no regard for the fact that I was married, and neither did the women who were throwing themselves at me; they just wanted to have their claim to fame. I justified hanging out with other women by saying that, if Andi didn't want to be a part of this life, there were many other women who did. Although I remained faithful in the beginning, living that way became lonely and dangerous and, in time, I gave in to the temptations surrounding me. Andi turned a blind eye to what was going on in New York during that year, and I acted like nothing was wrong. We stayed married and tried to convince our families—and ourselves—that we could live this way.

The season was going great, and I was in the lineup on a more regular basis. I got off to a very good start, and I knew it would be tough for Buck to get me more playing time. Our lineup was pretty well established and I wasn't one of the starters. Just when I was ready to start complaining again my fate turned, but only for a moment. Don Mattingly got injured and would be out of the lineup for at least four to six weeks. Finally, playing every day for Donnie allowed me to put up the numbers that I had been promising if I was ever given a full-time chance.

During these six weeks, I was leading the team in almost every offensive category. The media started reporting that Leyritz was finally backing up his bravado with his bat. Thinking this would be my break-out year, I was devastated when Donnie returned to lineup in early June and I returned to the bench. This was even more difficult than in the years past—I had actually proven myself and gotten a taste of what it was like to play every day. Unfortunately for me, the team was performing well, and none of the other starters got injured. Still, I had the best season of my entire career. I hit .309 with fourteen home runs and 53 RBIs with only 259 at-bats. My contract was up at the end of the year, and it was my first year of arbitration with the team.

When I returned to Fort Lauderdale in October, my marriage to Andi was all but over. I was seeing a girl named Karri while I was still legally married to Andi. I warranted the relationship by saying Andi and I were no longer intimate and would be divorcing soon. By December, 1993, I had filed for divorce. I look back now and realize I had sacrificed my most sacred relationship for my own selfish needs. Andi didn't deserve to be married to me for one more minute. I was not leading a God-driven life.

—◆—

When I got to the majors in 1990, I was using a thirty-three-inch, thirty-one-ounce bat, which was considered a small bat. But now it was 1993. The Yankees signed a guy named Danny Tartabull who used to use a big bat (thirty-five inches, thirty-three ounces.). Pat Kelly and I started borrowing his big bat in batting practice just for fun. Our hitting coach was six-foot-seven "Big" Frank Howard (known as "Hondo" when he played for the Washington Senators). He loved it. He told me and Pat we should be men and switch to a bigger bat. He felt a bigger and heavier bat would give us more power. In batting practice, we would kill the ball, but we would never use his big bat in a game—there was just no way we could get around fast enough with that war club.

On April 19, 1993, I faced Wilson Álvarez in Chicago. Still using my little thirty-three-inch bat, I got jammed twice. The third time I stood in to hit against him, Howard was standing near the bat rack during the game. He said, "Jumbo (one of my nicknames), you need to get this guy out of your kitchen. Why don't you use one of PK's BIG bats?" It can't be any worse than what you're doing now." The batter ahead of me got on base. Then the White Sox brought in Bobby Thigpen, one of the few relievers throwing 94–95 miles per hour. I walked back to the dugout and said to Howard, "Hondo, give me one of those big bats. I can't do any damage with this little bat." He shouted back, "All you have to do is get the head out." At the time, we were winning 7–3. Thigpen's first pitch was a ninety-three-miles-per-hour fastball. I fouled it straight back. Second pitch, same thing. I didn't think I could get the bat around in time to connect with one of his heaters. I worked the count to 3–2. On the next pitch, I took the easiest swing I could—and connected for my first grand slam in the majors. I continued to use that bat for the rest of the year.

My other grand slam was also off Thigpen in Seattle on April 27, 1994. In that game, the Mariner pitchers were horrible. They were walking hitters left and right. At one point, Mariners pitcher Jeff Nelson tried to hit me with a pitch out of frustration; he missed. In the top of the fifth inning, with Mike Gallego on third, Pat Kelly on second, and Randy Velarde on first, I came up against Thigpen and hit a grand slam. I literally walked around the bases. It was the longest home-run trot of my career, and one of the most enjoyable. When I touched home plate, I looked over at Mariners' manager Lou Piniella and said, "That one was for you!" We trounced the Mariners 12–2.

In the eighth inning, Gerald "Ice" Williams, a righty, had batted for Paul O'Neill, a lefty. The Yankees were up

11–2 at the time. Manager Lou Piniella really seemed to enjoy tormenting Paul O'Neill. O'Neill, who the Yankees' owner, George M. Steinbrenner III, once called his "warrior" because of his intensity on the field, hated striking out. Of course, no player likes to strike out, but after taking a called strike three, O'Neill would rant and fume in the dugout, banging and shouting at things. (One sportswriter said that O'Neill never struck out looking. The strike three calls were always wrong.)

After separating from Andi in 1994, I found an apartment in Fort Lauderdale where spring training would start the following February. Karri and I continued to date, and when camp was ready to break we decided we would continue to see each other. I really wanted a stable, healthy, and monogamous relationship. This time, I was determined not to let the big league lifestyle corrupt my morals and vowed never to make the same mistakes I had made in my last relationship.

Although my divorce was dragging on, Karri came up to New York frequently during the beginning of the season. Things were going well and we talked about her possibly moving up to New York before the season was over. I wanted to see if she could handle the pressures of the city and the baseball life. In June, Karri called late one night with some surprising news—I was going to be a father. The news put all of our plans into fast-forward, and the very next week she left her job and moved in with me. For some strange reason, even though we were not married, I felt that this was a blessing. But with my divorce still not final and a new baby on the way, I was very nervous about the changes ahead.

The year 1994 will forever be known as the "Strike Year." The bargaining agreement between the players union and the owners was set to expire at the end of the season. Negotiations began to break down in July. Without an agreement, we knew a work stoppage would be inevitable, but we never dreamed it would last the entire second half of the season and result in the cancellation of the entire postseason, including the World Series. I tried to stay in shape, hoping that somehow the season would resume. But it was not to be.

I hit a few home runs. One of my favorite homers was against Roger Clemens when he was in his prime with the Red Sox right before the strike of 1994. Roger Clemens is one of the greatest pitchers in history, with the most strikeouts in the history of the American League. It goes without saying that this is precisely why this is one of my favorite home-run memories! With one man aboard in the sixth, I took Clemens deep over the Green Monster nets in left field and onto the parking lot on Lansdowne Street. After I hit it, I watched it. Clemens turned around and stared at me, shouting, "What are you looking at?" I answered, "That!"

Later that year at one of our union meetings during the strike, Roger confronted me about my homer. He saw me and jokingly said, "Hey, you don't need to be standing and watching your home runs. You don't have that much time in [the major leagues]." I told him, "I don't hit balls like that every day. To hit one off you, in Fenway Park, where my boyhood team, the Reds, played the Reds Sox in the 1975 World Series, I *had* to watch that ball sail!" We both got a good laugh out of it. Throughout my career, I hit Clemens rather well: .385 (5/13). I later played with Roger in 1999 and got to catch him just once.

The 1994 strike made everything more difficult. Karri and I had gotten married at her house in North Miami on December 4, 1994, right before having our first son, Austin Michael Leyritz, on December 17, 1994. We had bought a new house in Clearwater, Florida, and we were way over our heads in bills. The strike had cost us three months of salary as well as the money we would have made for the play-offs. Also if we had finished the 1994 season, the extra days of service would have given me a huge raise in salary. I would have had enough at bats to be considered a full-time player. As a full-time player in arbitration, I would have gone from making $742,000 to almost $5 million. Instead, I was still considered a part-time player and was given a contract for $1.35 million.

As upset as I was at losing out on all that money, I knew the players after me would benefit from our union sticking together. I remember at the time the union told us we were doing the right thing, that someday in the future, players would be making $20 million per year. We laughed, because at the time, the highest-paid player was somewhere around $8 million, and we thought that was ridiculous.

We never played another game in 1994, and the strike caused the World Series to be canceled for the first time in baseball history. That was a very bad time for baseball and the fans. The fallout from the strike could have ruined baseball's popularity for a long, long time. The union and the owners eventually agreed on a new contract, and the spring training of 1995 would not be jeopardized.

6

The King

1995 was the beginning of the Yankees' drive to prominence. We knew that this was going to be Don Mattingly's last year and that there would be some changes in 1996. 1995 was a great year for the team but almost a setback for me personally. From 1993 to 1994, I had put up numbers that would compare to the best players in the game. The New York media continued to back me and we played much better baseball under Buck Showalter; we were in first or second place the entire year. Despite being upset about playing time again, I didn't say a word. The team was winning and that was the main goal. Still, I had many private meetings with Buck about sitting me more and more. He kept telling me I was more valuable on his bench than starting. This way he could use me when it mattered most. Buck had confidence that he could put me in the tough situations and I would come through for him.

The 1995 American League Division Series was Don Mattingly's first appearance in the postseason after fourteen stellar seasons as the Yankees' first baseman. It was also his last. He had a chronic bad back, and we knew he would not be back for the 1996 season. We all really wanted to win for him, and the whole city was rooting for Donnie.

We won Game 1 of the series against the Seattle Mariners at home in a 9–6 slugfest with David Cone getting the win.

Game 2 was also at Yankee Stadium. The Mariners were always tough, and there was no love lost between our two teams. Earlier that season, Randy Johnson had hit me in the head—I went down near home plate and the benches cleared. By the time I came to, the on-field fighting was over. As I walked down to first, I told Johnson I would be waiting for him after the game. I waited outside their clubhouse for more than an hour but he wouldn't come out. Finally, I was asked to leave by stadium security. On another occasion, the benches cleared again when Paul O'Neill and John Marzano got into a fight at home plate. So this series had a lot of piss and vinegar.

I was in the starting lineup for Game 2 on October 4, 1995. Manager Buck Showalter's decision to always save me for the clutch situations couldn't happen because he needed me to catch Andy Pettitte. I was Andy's personal catcher—the catcher he had the most confidence would call for the pitches he liked. The game was tied 4–4 in the seventh inning. Some of the bad blood between our teams started to boil. Bill Risley hit me in the back with a pitch. Even though it may not have been intentional, it added to the tension, which was already running high. The game remained tied until the twelfth inning. Ken Griffey Jr. hit a home run to put the Mariner's up 5–4. But in the bottom of the inning, Ruben Sierra drove in Jorge Posada, and Bernie Williams tried to score the winning run but was thrown out at the plate. Later, in the middle of the thirteenth inning with one out and Don Mattingly on second base, I grounded out to pitcher Tim Belcher. I was so mad at myself that I took it out on the water cooler and some bats. David Cone joked that he was surprised I had so much energy left after catching for thirteen innings.

We were still tied up in the bottom of the fifteenth

inning. Buck told me I had done a great job in this game, but that after my next at bat I was done. Fifteen innings was more than enough, and he was going to put Mike Stanley in behind the plate. His last words to me as I went to bat were, "Make it count."

It was raining when I stepped into the batter's box. With Pat Kelly on first, I battled Tim Belcher to a 3–2 count. The next pitch, I hit a two-run homer to win the game. The ball sailed over Jay Buhner's head in right field. Final score: Yankees 7, Mariners 5. Considering that it was the fifteenth inning, that it was a walk-off home run, and that it was against the Mariners, hitting that home run was the biggest thrill of my career—even greater than my game-tying home run in the World Series the next year.

The next day I sat. Again. Mike Stanley caught and homered. But the Mariners won 7–4. Seattle went on to win that Series 3–2, which was a crushing blow to the Yankees, who had very high expectations. We had been ahead 2–1 in a best of five series; but we lost. Don Mattingly retired after the season, never having appeared in a League Championship Series or World Series. We didn't know it at the time, but that was also Buck Showalter's last game as Yankee manager.

I grew up idolizing Mattingly, and I was disappointed that he never got to play a "final" game in Yankee Stadium in front of the New York fans who could applaud him for all he had given to them. We wanted to give Mattingly a proper send-off—a final at bat in front of fifty thousand adoring fans. But it wasn't to be. We lost to the Mariners, and Don's last at bat was 2,400 miles away from Yankee Stadium.

Donnie would be missed. I really enjoyed him as a teammate and friend. He taught me so much about the game. When he was hurt and not playing, he'd still come out and give me tips that he thought might help the team win that day. We spent a lot of time off the field talking about the game. He was "Donnie Baseball"—and he really earned the nickname. No other player I've ever been around was as humble or easily accessible as the Captain. He even gave me my nickname: the King.

After a few moves were made, the Yankees finally spoke to my agents. Once manager Buck Showalter was fired at the end of the 1995 season, I thought that my position as a bench player might finally change. Buck had always liked having me available to pinch-hit late in the game and probably would not have given me more at bats than the year before. If Buck had come back in 1996, I probably would have asked for a trade.

The hiring of former catcher Joe Torre gave me a glimmer of hope that my chances of getting more at bats and more playing time would finally change. When my agents spoke to Steinbrenner, that was the first question they asked. Torre told Steinbrenner he liked my versatility and told my agents that he thought he could get me

400 at bats, so I re-signed with the Yankees hoping for a more productive season in 1996. When I finally signed, after all the changes that were made, I had become the senior Yankee on the team in terms of length of service. I had more than six and a half years in the major leagues and four and a half in the minors—all in the Yankees organization.

The 1996 season was full of ups and downs, but in the end we won the American League Eastern Division two weeks before the season ended. I had a good year but still only had 250 at bats—this was the season Torre promised me I would have 400. This didn't bother me as much as it could have because we were winning and I had some special things happening in my personal life. Karri was pregnant with our second son, and, because we had clinched the division early, I would be able to be there for his birth. Our last series of the season was a weekend series against the Red Sox. The Yankees let me miss our Thursday and Friday games so I could be with Karri when she was induced. We scheduled it for Thursday because Torre wanted me back by Saturday to catch Andy Pettitte's last start before the playoffs began. Dakota James Leyritz was born on September 27, 1996. Four hours after his birth, I was on a train to Boston. Such is the life of a big leaguer during a crucial time in a season.

When it comes to home runs, the most important one I hit was in Game 4 of the World Series in Atlanta on

October 23, 1996. It was a critical game in the World Series and one of the most memorable World Series home runs in Yankees history. Some even say that that home run started the Yankees' dynasty of the late twentieth and early twenty-first century. It was also a turning point in my relationship with Steinbrenner.

The Yankees had not been in the Series since 1981 and hadn't won it since 1978. The 1996 team looked and felt different. The new manager was Joe Torre, who had been a very good catcher for eighteen years in the majors, spending some time at first and third bases. He was the National League MVP in 1971. A Brooklyn native, Joe had managed in New York before with the Mets from 1977–81, but this was his first time in the American League. He knew the New York media well, but he also managed a team that wasn't winning (the Mets). The Yankee team created by Buck Showalter and Gene Michael was poised to begin winning. The media was tough on the organization for hiring someone who hadn't had a winning record. In fact, during his playing career and his fifteen years as a big-league manager (Mets, Cardinals, and Braves), Torre had never been in the postseason. They even labeled him "Clueless Joe," but general manager Bob Watson felt he was the right man for the job. Don Zimmer, with fifty years of experience as a player, coach, and manager, was named the bench coach.

An aside here about Don Zimmer: When Torre became the Yankees' manager in 1996, he asked Zimmer—who had been in baseball since 1949 and in the big leagues as a player, coach, and manager since 1954 (when he was with the Brooklyn Dodgers)—to be his bench coach. Although the two barely knew each other, they became very close and worked very well together. My relationship with Zim was rocky in the beginning because Girardi was his guy. And Zim didn't like the fact that I had fun while playing, that I wasn't always serious. Plus, I liked to be challenged. Zim didn't want to push guys. He thought players should do the extra stuff on their own. I knew I wasn't going to catch any pitchers other than Andy Pettite, so I wouldn't go to the bull pen and catch all the other workdays for the other pitchers. Zimmer thought that I was lazy, but actually that is when I'd do my extra work practicing the different skills for other positions.

Zim wanted me catching in the bull pen more. That was the only thing Zim and I butted heads on. I respected him for all the knowledge he had from all his years in the game. Zim had the best job in the world. He got to make decisions Torre would use, but he didn't have to take responsibility for the outcome of those decisions.

There has never been a better combination of manager

and bench coach in the game: Torre, with his grace of handling people and personalities, and Zim, with all the baseball knowledge. It wasn't a coincidence that the Yankees weren't the same after he left in 2002. In my opinion, one of the few mistakes of George's final years was driving Zimmer away.

The other coaches that were hired all had great backgrounds, including postseason and World Series experience: Willie Randolph had been a great Yankee and outstanding second baseman. Mel Stottlemyre, a former pitching star with the Yankees, was the new pitching coach. Stottlemyre was very well respected by many in baseball. Former outfielder José Cardenal was also a good fit as the first base coach. This team was ready to win—it just needed the right man at the top. Joe Torre was in a very good spot. This team had some veterans like Paul O'Neill, Bernie Williams, and David Cone, and some good young talent, especially Derek Jeter, who was just coming up. Tino Martinez was acquired from Seattle to play first base, the position previously held by Don Mattingly. All of these things led Yankee fans to believe that 1996 would be a special year for the Yankees, a year in which they were sure to return to the World Series.

———

We were down two games to none and were headed to Atlanta for the next three. The Braves had gained an edge in the most important way: in morale. The Braves were glad to have won the first two games in the Bronx, and we felt that they were getting complacent. We could capitalize on that by doing to them in their house what they had done to us in ours. If the Braves won just two more games in Atlanta, it would all be over; they wouldn't have to return to New York.

We won Game 3. We were still alive. At our meeting before Game 4, all the players thought that if we could win this game, we could turn the entire Series around. It was no secret that the Braves didn't like playing in New York. Many teams shared this sentiment. New York fans are tough, and they are territorial when it comes to visitors winning in their park. They take it personally. They really put the heat on, and it's fantastic—when you're sitting in the home dugout! If we could get the Series back to New York, we'd have beaten them at their own game and we would have a chance to win it all.

Kenny Rogers was our starting pitcher in Game 4. Kenny had a rough year adjusting to the pressures of pitching in New York. Many Yankee fans were worried about Torre using him and thought he should be passed over. But Joe, who always gave his players an opportunity to prove themselves, gave Kenny the ball. This backfired almost immediately. By the fifth inning, we were losing 6–0. I remember turning to Pat Kelly in the dugout and saying, "At least we didn't get swept." Both of us figured this game was all but over. Torre paced up and down the dugout and tried to encourage the team to mount a comeback. The odds of us pulling it off against the Brave's great pitching staff were very slim. Finally, in the sixth inning we managed to score three runs. Now the game was 6–3. The game was on track to becoming the longest in World Series history (four hours, seventeen minutes). I had gone to the clubhouse and was watching the game on television while lifting weights, something bench players do to stay loose in case they're needed. Torre lifted Joe Girardi (future Yankees manager) for pinch-hitter Paul O'Neill, who struck out. With Girardi now out of the game and no other catcher besides me on the roster, I was all Torre had left. I went in to catch Jeff Nelson in the bottom of the sixth inning. When I came to bat in the eighth with one out, Mariano Duncan was on first and Charlie Hayes was on third. I had to face Braves closer Mark Wohlers before a crowd of more than 51,000 screaming fans and a worldwide TV and radio audience in the millions. If the Yankees had a third catcher on their roster, Torre would probably have had Wade Boggs pinch-hit for me, and then brought in the third catcher when we took the field in the bottom of the inning. Boggs was not in the game. He and Tino Martinez were out, and Cecil Fielder was in at first base, with Charlie Hayes at third.

As I walked to the plate, I thought of another adage

my dad used to say when he didn't want me to think too much about the pressure, "See the ball, hit the ball." I had never faced Wohlers before, but I knew his record as the top closer in the National League that year with thirty-three saves and an earned run average (ERA) of 3.03. I asked Don Zimmer in the on-deck circle what pitches Wohlers had. He replied, "Jimmy, the guy throws 100 miles per hour. Just go up there and be ready." I had borrowed Darryl Strawberry's bat because I wanted to save my two last bats for Game 5, which I was scheduled to start in the next day. Wohler's first pitch was a fastball. I fouled it straight back. He probably thought that I had his delivery timed, judging from my swing. Then came two nasty sliders up out of the strike zone. The next pitch was a fastball, which I again fouled back. Now the count was 2–2. The fifth pitch was a pretty good slider, but again, I fouled it off down the third base line.

I was thinking fastball, since I had two balls on his sliders, but Wohlers hung a slider out over the plate. I instantly made the adjustment, kept my hands back, and got enough of it to hit it into the left-field seats for a three-run home run. (Incidentally, that's the photograph on the cover of this book.) I had tied the game 6–6. As I rounded second base, all I could think about was that this game wasn't over. We still had to win it. I knew my home run was a pivotal moment but if we didn't win this one, it wouldn't mean anything. Just like the year before when

I hit the big home run in Game 2 of the playoffs against Seattle and we won the game but lost the series.

I found out later that Wohler's second-best pitch was not a slider but a forkball. I thought he just threw a fastball and a slider. Had I known that he had a forkball, I might have been looking for something different, especially since he hadn't thrown me any forkballs. On that swing, the momentum swung back in the Yankees' favor. My home run catapulted the Yankees back into the Series.

In the bottom of the eighth, the Braves went down with a force-out, a strikeout, and a groundout. Still 6–6. The game remained tied through the ninth inning. But in the top of the tenth, I grounded out, as did pitcher Graeme Lloyd. Tim Raines walked, and Derek Jeter singled him to second. An intentional walk of Bernie Williams by Braves pitcher Steve Avery loaded the bases with Raines on third and Jeter on second. Then Wade Boggs batted for Andy Fox and walked in a run. Now the score was 7–6 Yankees. Charlie Hayes then reached on an error that scored Derek Jeter. Now it was 8–6. Finally, Darryl Strawberry struck out to end the strange inning, with the Yankees still up by two. In the bottom of the inning, John Wetteland came in as the Yankees' closer. He put the victory away with a strikeout, a single, and two fly outs. Final score: Yankees 8, Braves 6. With the Series tied at two, we knew we would win the Series in Yankee Stadium. We no longer had to worry about the next day's game being an elimination game: win or go home. Our confidence soared.

To make that win even sweeter, this was the first time in their long history that the Yankees had come from six runs back to win a postseason game. As soon as the game was over, I was called into manager Joe Torre's office. He told me that even though I had caught Andy Pettitte all season long (Pettitte was 16–6 when I was behind the plate, and his teammates thought he was on his way to the Cy Young Award), I was not going to catch Game 5. Pettitte and I had a miserable loss in Game 1; Torre felt I didn't follow the scouting reports and that Andy was afraid to shake off the pitches I called. Game 5 was too important for us to lose and he didn't think I would follow the game plan. He said that I called pitches more by feeling than by scouting reports.

I told Torre, "That's fine, I don't really care. I just hit the biggest World Series home run in Yankee history. *You're* the one who will have to talk with the reporters about the lineup change." I walked out of his office, but before the reporters came into the Yankees' clubhouse to ask me about the home run, Torre changed his mind. He called me back to say that I would catch Pettitte in Game 5, but that I needed to follow his game plan.

I'm not quite sure what changed Torre's mind. Pettitte didn't blame the devastating loss on me. We worked as a team, and even though I called the pitches, Andy hadn't shaken any of them off either. Pitchers have that right. This fact might have influenced Torre, and maybe Andy knew that and spoke to him on my behalf. I never asked Torre why he changed his mind. I just wanted to play. In Game 1, we were beaten because we didn't make the right pitches. But if given the opportunity in Game 5, we'd go out and do the right thing.

That night I went home and celebrated the home run with my friends and family. The next morning I received dozens of phone calls from newspapers across the country wanting me to describe the significance of my home run in changing the momentum of the World Series. Eventually, I'd had enough. After all, how thrilled can you sound after the fiftieth call? (Even though, of course, I was.) But the last call I took, was much more important. The caller, a reporter for the *New York Post*, quickly said that she wasn't calling about my home run. She was calling to let me know that the two orphaned brothers I'd sponsored and for whom I'd been trying to find a permanent home had finally been legally adopted!

The glory of hitting a home run in the World Series was my dream, but it paled in comparison to this meaningful news. In June 1996, the *Post* ran a story about the city's adoption-month program, which included these boys. Their picture appeared on page one beneath the headline: We Want a Daddy to Take Us to a Yankee Game. Karri, who was then pregnant with our second son, got us involved. We contacted the boys through the paper and hoped to take them to a Yankee game. With the help of Nicholas Scarpetta, then the head of the city's Children's Services Agency, we set up a day that we hoped the boys would never forget: a pick up at their foster home in a limousine and lunch at the All Star Café, followed by a visit to the Yankee locker room. Though the boys were just nine and six at the time, and I knew how thrilling it would be for them to meet all of the Yankees.

During the broadcast of the game, MSG, then the Yankees' TV outlet, showed a piece about the boys' special day, which included a phone number for anyone interested in adopting them. Seventeen calls came to the Yankees organization that night during the game! At the end of the day, Steven, the oldest boy, asked if I could be his daddy. I told him that while that wasn't possible, I would be his friend for life. In September, Karri and I hosted a charity event to kick off a foundation for the Children's Services Agency. Twenty-three Yankees acted as waiters and bartenders. Even Mayor Giuliani, a huge Yankees fan, showed up to lend support. We raised close to $100,000 dollars that night.

I will always believe that God's blessing was with me on October 23, 1996, the day I walked to the plate to take what would be the most important at bat of my life. The same day that would turn out to be monumental, both for me and for two boys who now had a family.

On my way to the ballpark before Game 5, I remember feeling elated. After all, I'd just hit a historic home run, and my two young orphan friends had finally found a family. Game 5 was a return to reality. Joe Torre, who put my name in the lineup behind the plate, was now challenging me to do a better job of calling the game than I had in Game 1.

In Game 5, the last game ever played at Atlanta's Fulton County Stadium, Pettitte pitched a 1–0 shutout. That was the greatest game I've ever played in. Even more suspenseful and pivotal than the home run game, Game 5 came down to the last pitch in the bottom of the ninth inning with the tying run on third base. Our closer, John Wetteland, threw seven or eight fastballs in a row to pinch-hitter Luis Polonia. Wetteland called me out to the mound and asked what I thought about a curveball. I told him, "Absolutely not! Wohlers got beaten last night on his *second*-best pitch. *You're* not going to get beaten on your *second*-best pitch!" If we were going to get beaten, it would be with Wetteland's best pitch—his fastball. He threw it, and Polonia hit a line drive toward the right center field gap. Paul O'Neill, who had just been moved over a few steps in the gap by outfield coach José Cardenal, made a great play on the ball. Had Paul not moved over he wouldn't have been in position to make the catch. This was just another example that every move our team made in that series seemed to be the right one. Paul caught the ball and we now led the

Series 3–2. The momentum had switched to the Yankees and we were headed to the Bronx.

I take more pride in Game 5 of that series than I do in the home run in Game 4. The home run game was given to me by chance, but Game 5 was a challenge given to me by Joe Torre, a former catcher. Joe works well with players, which is why he's such a terrific manager. He figured me out. If I had a challenge, I'd rise to it. When Joe told me that he thought the loss of Game 1 was my fault, I wanted to prove him wrong. I also stole a base in Game 5. What a thrill! In my whole career, I stole only seven bases. How many catchers can say, "I stole a base in the World Series"?

Game 6 was crazy. The momentum that we created by winning all three games in Atlanta had erupted throughout Yankee Stadium. The fans had completely forgotten about our dismal performances in Games 1 and 2 and the stadium was rocking with the knowledge that we were on the brink of bringing the championship home. Even though I was on the bench, Game 6 was one of the most exciting games I have ever witnessed. When Joe Girardi tripled and drove in the game's first run, the noise level at Yankee Stadium was the loudest I had ever heard. The crowd went wild and we were pumped. We scored two more runs to make it 3–0 and everyone was on their feet from that moment on. The last inning was a nail-biter. The Braves closed the gap to 3–2 and with two outs remaining, Mark Lemke came up to bat. He worked the count full and John Wetteland's next pitch was popped up along the third base dugout. Third baseman Charlie Hayes just barely missed catching the foul pop-up near the Braves' dugout. The next pitch was almost a déjà vu, except this time Hayes was able to make the catch. We won the game 3–2. It was the Yankees' first world championship since 1978. The team piled on the mound and we all went nuts. Torre and the other coaches joined us at the mound and Joe told all the guys to take a lap around the field. He wanted us to share our moment with the greatest and most loyal fans in baseball.

The 1996 off-season was incredible. I had made my mark in Yankee history. Our team received all types of awards for winning the Series and I was on cloud nine. The mayor even gave each of us the key to the city. As I was basking in the glory of my own success, God reminded me, as always, that there are other things in life more important than baseball. In November of 1996, we got a phone call from the adopted boys. They wanted Karri and me to come up for their official adoption ceremony and be there for this special day. We flew up to New York and went to the courthouse. We were escorted into a meeting room where Ms. Cortes, the adoptive mother, was signing papers. Eric and Steven Cortes would be the boys' new names. They would finally have the security of someone in their lives and a home to wake up in every

day. Then something happened that still makes me cry
every time I talk about it. The oldest boy, Steven, stood
up and started to speak. He said he wanted to give Karri
and me a necklace that he and Eric would also wear. It
was a pendant bearing the number 13 on a chain. A hush
came over the room. As if that wasn't enough, he turned
to me and said "Jim, thank you for giving me a family,
and if you will allow me, I would like to change my name
officially to JIMMY LEYRITZ CORTES." For the first
time in my boisterous life, I was speechless. I sat down
and just started to cry. I told him of course he could and
it would be my honor for him to include my name in his.
God truly had worked a special miracle in my life that
year and it wasn't baseball. Today, Steven (twenty-four)
resides in New York with his girlfriend and Eric (twenty-
one) is in the Army. Unfortunately, Ms. Cortes passed
away a few years back. Steven and I are still in touch and
I visit him often when I'm in New York.

7

Full-time Status

Months later, the city was still buzzing after the Yanks won the World Series against the Braves. I thought that the remarkable Game 5 I caught with Andy, as well as my Game 4 hit (the most talked-about play of the postseason), should finally earn me what I had been striving for since high school: a full-time starting position. I committed more than seven years to the Yankees organization, proving myself over and over, rising to challenges, taking demotions, clashing with managers, and being shuffled between Single A and Double A. What more could I do to demonstrate my heart, my loyalty, and my ability to perform? Let's face it: you can't play solely on heart—at least for the Yankees. At some point you need to perform. And I thought that's what I did. Tickertape fell from the sky in October—tangible proof that I *had* performed. Play me already. I was the toast of New York—but would I still be a Yankee?

I didn't get to where I got in my career by being easily satisfied. If I didn't have heart or ambition, I might still be catching in Single A, making a livable salary playing a game that I loved. But I wanted more. I wanted the big leagues, I wanted to win, and I wanted a ring. I got all three, but that hunger came creeping up again. I wanted to be a *full-time* catcher. No more of this backup catcher rotation garbage. Play me or trade me. And that's exactly what I told Steinbrenner in early 1997.

As much as my 1996 home run meant to the Yankees in terms of helping to win the World Series and revive their dynasty, it helped free me to make some other tough decisions. I knew it was time to fulfill my dream of becoming a full-time player—not just a benchwarmer—in New York or elsewhere.

I told my agents, Tom Reich and Adam Katz, that I had been with the Yankees for seven years. I'd given the

Yankees everything I had. I'd been a part-time player, and I put up good numbers in 1993 and 1994. I thought with the World Series home run and the way I caught Andy Pettitte in Game 5, I had finally earned the right to demand a role as a full-time player. I told Adam and Tom that if the Yankees wouldn't give me a full-time role, they should start looking elsewhere.

Steinbrenner said he couldn't commit to making the decision about me going full-time yet, because he didn't know what was going to happen with their first-string catcher, Joe Girardi. Joe was a free agent, meaning that he could sign with any team he wanted to. Torre said that the Yankees were going to spend the money to pursue and sign Girardi, and that they had switch-hitting Jorge Posada waiting in the wings. (The Yankees planned to develop him into a full-time catcher. Posada had played in only a handful of games in 1995 and 1996.) If I stayed, I'd probably have the same role in 1997 as I had in 1996—a little catching, a little first base, and a little time as the team's designated hitter with about 250 at bats.

Once I heard that, I instructed my agents to find me a team where I would be a starter. Sure, I loved the Yankees—they'd given me the chance to reach my dream of playing in the big leagues and my family and I liked living in New York City. But I wanted to play full-time, and that was just not going to happen in New York.

We needed and obtained Steinbrenner's permission

to talk with other clubs. Adam spoke with the Anaheim Angels general manager Bill Bavasi (son of former general manager Buzzie Bavasi). If the trade could be made, the Angels would offer me my first multiyear contract as a starter with some security: two years plus an option.

Once the trade with the Angels was made, I went to Steinbrenner's office in the Yankees complex in Tampa to thank him for giving me the opportunity to play in the majors, and for the Yankees. I thanked him for allowing me to be traded to the Angels where I would become a full-time player and a starter. I also thanked Steinbrenner for the use of the Yankees' training facilities in the off-season while I was a Yankee. I mentioned that I was going to move to Fort Lauderdale, and that I'd find someplace there to work out. I said I hoped to see him again sometime. He looked at me, surprised. He asked, "What are you talking about?" I said, "Now that I'm no longer a Yankee, I'm sure you don't want me working out at the Yankees complex." He looked at me and said, "Jimmy, for what you've done for this team and this organization, you will *always* be a Yankee. No matter what you do, no matter where you go: you'll always be welcome here. You started something special here." At the time, none of us could have known exactly what I had started or how long it would last—the Yankees dynasty and the Joe Torre years (1996–2007, including four world championships). Steinbrenner told me that I could work out at the

Yankees' Tampa facilities as long as I liked. He thanked
me and wished me the best of luck—*except* when I played
against the Yankees. We shook hands and I walked out
feeling great.

—◂ ◂—

Our family stayed in Tampa during the off-season and
I worked out at the Yankees' facilities to get in shape for
the season. The Yankee complex had full-time coaches
to throw batting practice and help the players. No other
teams had this kind of facility. We took batting practice
every day and then took ground balls—almost like getting a head start on spring training. By doing this, we
wouldn't have to go through the usual soreness a player
gets the first few days of spring camp. I remember Trey
Hillman was one of the coaches, and he used to do everything for us. After the fielding practice, we would use the
weight room to finish off our workouts.

Second baseman Pat Kelly, young shortstop Derek
Jeter, and some other players also worked out there in
the winter. It was strange, in a way, because I was going
to another team, yet Steinbrenner made me feel I would
always be a Yankee.

When I arrived at the Angels' spring training camp in
Arizona in February, I was extremely excited. It was great
to feel like I'd finally found some security in baseball after

seven years of one-year contracts, never knowing what the next year would hold. I was now a full-time player with a multiyear contract with a guarantee of a job with a big-league salary for at least the next two years.

I walked into the clubhouse and shook hands with manager Terry Collins and two guys I had idolized as a kid: coaches Larry Bowa and Dave Parker. I didn't know much about Collins. I told him I was looking forward to my first season as an everyday player and finally putting up the numbers I could only project before. I was going to have the chance to back up all my big words. He said, "Let's get you going—it's what you always wanted." After seven years in the majors, this was my first season in which I could concentrate on playing without having to worry about making the team. I was confident.

I did things I hadn't been able to do when I was just trying to make a team. Now I could concentrate on getting ready for the regular season. I didn't have to worry about my stats during the spring. For example, I used a forty-ounce bat during spring training, heavier than I would use during the season. With a heavy bat, you can't overswing. I used it to improve my bat speed. This was a tip that Frank Howard gave me when I used to work with him in spring training with the Yankees. Some ballplayers loosen up before stepping up to the plate by swinging two bats, a sledgehammer, or a bat with a heavy metal doughnut attached, so that when they step up to the plate with just *one* bat, they can bring the bat head around faster. I preferred warming up with a heavy bat. I was sure that this was going to be the season when I'd get the 400–500 at bats that I'd always relished.

I felt very comfortable with my three-year contract with the Angels. Karri and I found a beautiful house in Anaheim Hills, a short drive from the stadium. We were both so relieved that we wouldn't have to move every year. We were excited to put down roots and settle in Southern California. Austin was three and Dakota was sixteen months old. We were looking forward to starting a new life there and continuing the charity work that we had started in New York.

The year 1997 was the first year that the Disney Corporation owned the Angels. They did a lot of promotion for the team, much of it featuring me. We spent eight fun weeks at spring training with the Angels in Arizona. By the time we broke camp and returned to Anaheim to start the regular season, I was one of the team leaders, a veteran who had won a world championship. That earned me a lot of respect in the clubhouse. The team featured future Hall of Famer Eddie Murray, by then a designated hitter. Our kids loved living in California. They had a view of the mountains and a pool in the backyard. Karri and I had hired some part-time help (a housekeeper/babysitter), so sometimes after a home game we'd leave the kids with her and go out for dinner, just the two of us.

I was really looking forward to being the starting catcher for the first time in my career. But up ahead, as had become a pattern in my life, there was another unforeseen bump in the road. About a week before spring training ended, Terry Collins and third-base coach Larry Bowa asked me when I was going to turn it on at the plate. I assured them that once the season started on April 2, I'd be ready. Bowa, who had managed the Padres, said, "Jimmy, it's not like a switch. You can't just turn it on." I told him to look at my statistics from previous seasons. "I know how to put up great numbers." The last week of spring training, I started to use my own bats, and I hit four home runs. I told Bowa, "See? I can flip the switch just like that!" We broke camp and headed to Anaheim to get ready for Opening Day. Even though I knew that Bowa realized what I could do, I wasn't sure about the Angels' manager, Terry Collins. We had a workout in Anaheim the day before the season would begin. I had read a newspaper article that morning about the upcoming season. In it, Collins said that I would possibly be platooned with Jorge Fábregas behind the plate for the Angels, at least until he could tell how things worked out. I thought, *Here we go again.* Another empty promise made and I would be the one to pay the price. As someone who holds people to their words, I walked into Collins's office and showed him the article. I asked, "What the f--- is this all about?" Collins said, "You didn't have a great spring. I don't know what I'm going to do yet. I'm thinking of platooning you."

I reminded him of the conversation we had when we were first introduced: "Hi, Terry, I'm Jim Leyritz, your starting catcher. I'm looking forward to backing up my words and putting up big numbers now that I am an every-day player." I told him that when I was brought to the Angels, I was told that I would be the *full-time* catcher. I didn't think I had to compete with anybody for the number one catcher's spot. So I planned my spring training regimen with that in mind—to be ready to go on April 1. No one had indicated that there would be any changes to my starting position all spring, so I naturally assumed all was on course for my first full season.

I asked Collins to at least give me the month of April. I told him that if by the end of April he wasn't satisfied with my performance—if I wasn't putting up the numbers—he could do whatever he wanted, such as bench me or replace me with Fábregas. I had a lot of confidence in my ability. I had prepared well in spring training, and I *knew* I was ready to play. Collins agreed to give me a shot.

Our first game of the season was against the Boston Red Sox at home before a crowd of nearly 31,000. I started and batted eighth. My wife and my parents were there. I caught Mark Langston. I singled and scored a run before being replaced by Fábregas in the ninth inning, but the Red Sox won 6–5. The next day, the crowd was down to only 17,000.

Fábregas started behind the plate, and we won.

In the sixth game of the season, we faced the New York Yankees. It was strange taking batting practice in pinstripes, but not Yankee pinstripes. Then all of my former teammates came out in their road gray uniforms, and I said my hellos and spoke with the guys for a while. It was strange seeing them and actually preparing to play against them. I joked with Andy Pettitte, who was pitching in that series, that when I came to bat against him, I'd tell him what to throw. Since I'd been his "personal" catcher the year before, I said I'd know what was coming.

In the first game, the Yankees were leading 4–3 in the eighth inning when Mariano Rivera, perhaps the best relief pitcher of all time, came on in relief of setup man Mike Stanton. Darren Erstad was on third base. As I walked up to the plate, I heard, "Leyritz! Leyritz!"

Someone was screaming at me. Third base coach Larry Bowa pointed toward the dugout. Jack Howell, a left-handed hitter, had come out of the dugout and was walking toward the plate to pinch-hit for me. I was stunned. I looked at Terry Collins and asked, "What? Are you kidding me?"

Howell, a very good pinch-hitter, kept walking toward the plate. Me being me, I dropped my bat in disgust, walked into the dugout, and threw my helmet down. Everyone on the bench was looking at me, waiting to hear my reaction to being pinch-hit for in a crucial situation.

As I walked toward the clubhouse tunnel, I asked Collins, "Have you ever heard of Mark Wohlers?" Then I walked into the clubhouse. Terry didn't think it was funny, but my teammates got a chuckle out of it.

Cocky? Yes. Confident? Yes. Probably not the smartest thing to do to the manager, especially for a new guy on the team. But I was very upset; I thought this was to be my year. Wasn't I brought to Anaheim for situations like this? I couldn't believe that Collins would take me out in that situation. I had caught Mariano for two years, so I knew what he might throw. I also knew that left-handed hitters didn't do as well against him as righties. As it happened, Mariano struck Howell out, and the Yankees went on to win the game 5–3.

I had a meeting with Collins the next day, and I told him exactly how I felt. He said okay, that he understood and respected me for it. But he told me never to show him up like that again. I agreed, but emphasized that I was there to perform, not to be lifted for a pinch-hitter in a crucial situation.

The next night, Rivera came in to pitch the ninth inning with no outs and nobody on base. I came up to bat. Collins didn't pinch-hit for me. (Perhaps because I had homered in the second inning.) I looked over my shoulder just in case, but this time Collins was going to let me try to back up my big talk. I worked the count and smacked a hit to right field. As I got to first base, Dave Parker, our first base coach, gave me a high five. I asked him to look into the dugout and give Collins a "What were you thinking last night?" expression. He did so, and when I got back to the dugout, I said, "See? I could have tied that game up last night." We had a good laugh over it. The Angels won that game 10–9 in twelve innings.

I thought Terry finally realized who I was and what I could do. The bigger the situation, the more I wanted to be the guy at the plate. A man of his word, he gave me April to prove myself to him and to the team. By the end of the month, I was hitting .348 with four home runs, nineteen RBI's, and sixteen runs scored. I was thankful that Terry and the Angel organization gave me a chance.

Collins was interviewed again toward the end of the month by an Orange County newspaper, and he discussed the Angels' catching situation. He said that I had surprised him and a lot of others by the tremendous contributions I had made both at the plate and behind it. He was quoted as saying, "Jimmy has done a tremendous job hitting but has also done a good job handling the pitching staff. He is our starting catcher." It was great to finally see those words in print: *STARTING CATCHER.*

By July, we were in first place in the American League West. But pitcher Mark Langston went down with an elbow injury, and another frontline pitcher, Chuck Finley, suffered a shoulder injury. They were our number one and number two pitchers. By then, Jorge Fábregas had been traded to the White Sox. We had a new backup catcher named Todd Green. We needed pitching and we knew that management was searching for it. On July 29, the baseball world showed me again that anything could happen. We were in Cleveland, the city where I was born, playing the Indians. We were in first place and had a great chance to make the post season. This was everything Karri and I had wished for. My parents had come into town with my brother and sister and their families. I also left tickets for twenty to thirty of my aunts, uncles, and cousins who wanted to attend the game. My family and I had just finished lunch and were walking back into the hotel room when the telephone rang. I picked it up casually not knowing that the reality of baseball was about to rear its ugly head; players are a commodity to be traded and exchanged at any time and without any warning.

The call was from Tim Mead, head of the Angels Media Relations. He informed me I had been traded the Texas Rangers for Ken Hill who, at the time, was the Rangers number one starter. (The Angels later sent Rob Sasser to Texas to complete the deal.) I almost dropped the phone. The security of the place I thought I would call home for at least the next two years was suddenly pulled out from under me. Tim informed me that the Rangers were trading their catcher, Pudge Rodríguez to the New York Yankees for Jorge Posada, and I would still be starting catcher for the Rangers; Jorge would be my backup. That made it a little easier to accept the trade, but I still didn't want to go. I told my family the news and we were all in shock. Karri was angry but waited until we were alone to blame me for the trade. In the meantime, all of my relatives who I had left tickets for wondered why I wasn't on the field with the Angels taking batting practice. My dad got a hold of one of my aunts to let her know what happened. I went to the stadium and said my good-byes. It was very emotional. I had requested the trade from the Yankees to the Angels, but this trade hit me hard. I don't think the Angels really wanted to trade me, but with the injuries to Langston and Finley, I think I was the only one who had the value to get them the starting pitcher they needed. So I was gone. Some of the players were angry and didn't like the trade. Jim Edmonds even wore my number on his helmet that night as a tribute to me.

I spent that night in the Cleveland hotel with a heavy heart. Karri was furious and told me for the first time that she didn't think she could handle this baseball lifestyle. She went back to Anaheim to pack up the entire house with two young boys in tow while I headed out to Texas on a plane. Although still very disappointed to be leaving Anaheim, I thanked God that at least I was not losing my role as a starting catcher.

I still had my Angels suitcase when I got off the plane in Texas on July 30. Somebody saw it in the airport and recognized me. He said, "You're Jim Leyritz, right?" I said that I was. Then he asked me if I had heard the great news: Rodríguez had re-signed with the Rangers.

I said, "What?" The Rangers fan informed me that just before the trading deadline, Rodríguez had fired his agent, walked into the general manager's office by himself, and signed a five-year, $45 million contract. I was in shock—*You've got to be kidding me!*

I'd planned to stay in Anaheim for a few years and was blown away by the trade to the Rangers. But I thought that I'd be replacing a legend (Rodríguez came up to the Rangers in 1991 when he was just nineteen, and caught an average of 116 games per season), so when I first got traded being the starting catcher for the Rangers wasn't that bad. Now, another bump in the road. I was back in the same situation that I dreaded most—Pudge was the best catcher in the game at this time, so I knew where my place would be. Once again, I'd be the fill-in, the backup: Seinfeld's Kramer. Just what I didn't want, just what I'd left the security of the Yankee organization to get away from.

Karri showed up with the kids the following week and we got an apartment in Arlington. This was a big change from our beautiful house in Anaheim Hills. I wasn't happy with my playing position and she wasn't happy about having to pick up and move again. Things between us began to go downhill. She was still angry and wanted to know why this had happened. She asked me if I did something to the Angels that would "make them get rid of you?" I explained to her that unfortunately this was just the way baseball works. I don't think she understood that I didn't have enough seniority in the majors to veto the trade. (Under the rules negotiated by the players union, only a player who has been in the majors for ten years, including at least five with the same team, can veto a trade.) I just didn't have enough time in. Because I wasn't a superstar, my job security would always be up in the air. And now it looked like maybe another marriage would be, too.

Catchers usually make the best managers, and Rangers' manager Johnny Oates was no exception. Oates told me that he understood the difficult position I was in. He had been the backup catcher to Rick Cerone on the Yankees. He knew that I thought I was good enough to be some team's starting catcher. He said he knew the goals I had and the strides I'd made to reach them, only to lose control of my own destiny once again (which I naively thought I possessed). Oates said he'd try to get me as many at bats as he could by using me at different positions. But it was my misfortune to be traded to a team that had just re-signed Rodríguez to a five-year contract. Being a backup catcher to Rodríguez is like playing basketball for the Washington Generals, the Harlem Globetrotters' perennial opponents.

Johnny kept his promise and got me as many at bats as he could. I put up good numbers in my limited role with the Rangers but only got 85 at bats and hit .282 with 14 RBIs. Toward the end of the season, I injured my left knee in a play at the plate. I think the strain of the entire season contributed to my knee injury. This was my second surgery on my left knee. The first was ten years before during rookie ball in Oneonta. Catchers probably have more knee operations per years of service than any other players.

I left the team with fifteen days remaining in the season and went home to have some cartilage removed—nothing painful. Then I started rehabbing my knee. I could probably have limped along without the surgery, but I was afraid that I might hurt some other part of my knee, and I didn't want that. I wanted to be ready for a trade to a new team. I knew I wasn't going back to Texas. I thought, *If I can't help this team, I'm not going to risk further injury for possible future earnings.*

The 1997 off-season was my second surgery since I was in the big leagues. But I wasn't too discouraged, because I thought that during my stay in Anaheim, I'd put up good enough numbers to show that I deserved to be a starting catcher (eleven home runs and fifty RBIs in eighty-four games, about half a full season). My numbers projected to twenty to twenty-five home runs and more than a hundred RBIs for a full season, if I had enough at bats. The question was, where?

So instead of being home with Karri and the boys, I had to get up and go to rehab, work out, and do my physical therapy. This is when Karri realized that we could no longer use the four months in the off-season to do whatever we wanted—those days were over. Up to this point, I had been lucky: as a utility player, I wasn't playing every day and we could live a little during the season, especially during the winter. But now I had to use the off-season to get myself ready to be an everyday player. She was finding out that because I was not an Alex Rodriguez or a Derek Jeter, I had to earn my place on the team every year. There were no guarantees for me. We had to sacrifice what had been our free time in the off-season to be ready for me to be an everyday player come Opening Day. I had to train every day during the off-season. She also didn't like the fact that every time I got traded she was the one left having to pick up all of the pieces. This was an arduous task with two small children to care for—one she would have to repeat often.

Our marriage started to fall apart. We began spending less quality time together. I was busy rehabbing and spending any free time I had with the boys. She was busy socializing with friends and began to go out at night without me.

———

After the nightmare in Texas, my agents brokered a deal to send me to the Boston Red Sox in a five-player deal. Out-

fielder Damon Buford and I went to Boston for pitchers
Mark Brandenburg and Aaron Sele, and catcher Bill Hasel-
man. Finally, I would be the starting catcher on a team
in the American League East, where baseball was more of
a passion than it was out west. In my view, the American
League East was the best division in the majors.

I was excited to be playing in Boston. If you went 0–4
for one of the West Coast teams, the fans didn't really
care. You'd do better next time. But if you went 0–4 in
Boston or New York, the fans really let you hear it. In
these places, you're only as good as your last at bat. I was
looking forward to getting back to that. It reminded me
of the days when my father was coaching me: three-for-
four just wasn't good enough. I liked playing where the
fans never let you have a letdown.

The Red Sox made me feel wanted. They had seen what
I did in Anaheim and assured me that I was the answer to
helping them get back to the playoffs, which they had not
been able to reach the previous few years.

Being traded to the Red Sox in 1998 reminded me that
it really didn't matter who you played for. One day to the
next, there isn't a lot of loyalty in baseball: you just go
out on the field and try to perform the best you can every
day God gives you the opportunity. I stayed focused on
the fact that being a major-league baseball player was different from most other jobs: millions of people all across
the country dreamed of having my job, and there were

only 780 players in the big leagues. This helped me stay grounded and underscored my faith and my self-confidence on the field.

Spring training in 1998 would bring a lot of new changes to my life both personally and professionally. On the personal side, Karri had informed me that for the first time she wanted to stay home in Fort Lauderdale with the boys during training. She explained that one of her close friends had just lost his wife to a brain aneurysm and she wanted to lend him support. He was struggling with his children and she felt our boys could help his kids cope with their tremendous loss. My gut gnawed at me, but I knew this was a spring that I needed to really focus on my job. I ignored the fact that Matt was a former boyfriend and I convinced myself that Karri was just being a good friend. Professionally, as a former Yankee, it was a pleasant surprise to be welcomed into the Red Sox clubhouse for spring training.

Jimy Williams, a well-respected baseball man, was the manager and Joe Kerrigan was the pitching coach. There was no animosity, even though I'd played for Boston's longtime rival in the American League East. I knew some of the players, such as John Valentin and Mo Vaughn, and I thought I fit in well with the team. Jason Varitek had just signed with the Sox, and I thought I would do most of the catching while teaching him the ropes, just as Joe Girardi was doing with Jorge Posada on the Yankees.

The Sox had another catcher, Scott Hatteberg. I thought I could help tutor both Varitek and Hatteberg while possibly playing a few other positions. Kerrigan and I talked about our different styles and strategies. He said he wanted me to look into the dugout before every pitch; he was going to call every pitch, as they do in college. I was shocked and asked why. I wasn't an inexperienced catcher like Varitek and Hatteberg who may need his help. I'd caught in the major leagues for seven years. I knew how to call a game.

"Wait a minute," I said. "Don't the Red Sox have team meetings before each game or before each series to go over pitches? We have Pedro Martinez, Bret Saberhagen [both of whom had won the Cy Young Award] and knuckle-baller Tim Wakefield. They're veterans who are going to call their own games." We also had two young pitchers on the staff—John Wasdin and Derek Lowe. I think those are the guys he wanted to call the pitches for.

As I found out later, Kerrigan was a control freak as well as a pipeline: Whatever players said to one another in the clubhouse went right through him to management. He was a squealer. Private observations and conversations he overheard were immediately reported to the manager. This was another side of Kerrigan that I didn't like. (Some former players informed me that Williams found out later that he wasn't immune to Kerrigan's interference. He discovered that Kerrigan was going behind his back to the Sox front office, eventually getting him fired in 2001. Williams's successor as manager of the Boston Red Sox? Joe Kerrigan. There was a method to Kerrigan's madness.)

On the issue of calling the pitches, Kerrigan and I just didn't see eye-to-eye, so I discussed it with the manager, Jimy Williams. He said we'd see what happened as spring training progressed. The next weekend Karri and the boys came to visit me at the spring training apartment in Fort Myers. During her stay, she seemed very distant and the boys told me that her friend Matt had been spending a lot of time at our house. I knew something wasn't right when I asked her how Matt was coping. I was trying to gauge how much longer she thought she would need to stay in Fort Lauderdale before she and the boys would be joining me. Her response was, "I need a little more time."

Karri had left a few bags in the apartment to reassure me she would be coming back soon. Ironically, two days later our nanny called to tell me that Karri and Matt seemed to be more than just friends. She told me she didn't want to get involved but urged me to look into Karri's bag for a love letter and necklace supposedly given to her by Matt. Sure enough, when I looked through one of the bags I found exactly what she had described. I wasn't completely surprised, and to this day believe she left those items for me to find on purpose, but it still hurt to find out the truth. I wanted to wait and confront her in person and quickly went into Williams' office. I told him I was having personal problems and needed to go home for two days. He was not happy to have me leave but I was upfront with him about what was happening, and he approved it. Soon, two days turned into eight days. Karri tried to explain her way out of it. She blamed Matt and said he was the one pursuing her and that nothing had ever happened. I didn't know what to believe and I told her I wanted her and the boys with me in Fort Myers as soon as possible.

When I returned to the team, I spoke with Williams and told him I had handled the situation and that I wouldn't have to leave again. The timing was terrible. Karri never admitted to being unfaithful but in my heart, I knew better. I did a lot of praying, and in the end, decided to forgive her and try to make our marriage work. I knew the life of a baseball wife could be extremely difficult. Our boys deserved a family and I did not want to go through another painful divorce. The good news was that she and the boys joined me for the last few weeks of training. The bad news was that because of the time that I missed, I never got to work out my differences with Kerrigan.

When the Red Sox broke camp at the end of spring training, I was no longer a catcher. I had missed too much time, and I had had a huge fight with Joe Kerrigan over who would call pitches during games. Also, Jason Varitek had a very good spring. The team planned to use Varitek and Hatteberg behind the plate. I was to be the designated hitter against left-handed pitchers, with Reggie Jefferson being the designated hitter against righties. I wasn't happy about this decision, but I couldn't say much, because my own personal problems had cost me my job. I decided I would see how things would work out once the season started.

It started out pretty good. I hit eight home runs in the first two months of the season, and Karri and I were making it work. Nevertheless, by June I wasn't playing much. I asked Williams for more playing time. If I was not going to get it, I was going to ask for a trade. A player who was traded in the middle of a multiyear contract can ask for a trade, and you can't put up numbers sitting on the bench. About a week later, I was called into Williams' office. The Red Sox had hired private detectives to check up on players, including the eight of us who lived in Waltham.

One of the detectives reported that Karri had repeatedly entered a costume store and was possibly buying drugs while our kids were with her. I was shocked by this accusation. I asked, "Are you kidding me?" My kids liked to look at the Halloween masks and costumes. I had been there once or twice myself. I didn't think anything of it at the time. I thought it was completely innocent. But Jimy Williams and general manager Dan Duquette told me they believed it was more than that. They told me to be careful. I confronted Karri and she was adamant that there was absolutely no truth to those accusations. I had never seen any evidence of her using or abusing drugs, and thought this was just a ploy by the team to get me to back down from my request to be traded. (I found out later from Karri's mother that she had been in a drug-treatment facility as a teenager, and she had never told me.) I still demanded a trade.

Finally, Reich and Katz were able to negotiate a trade for me to San Diego. The Padres had just lost their backup catcher, Greg Myers, to an injury. Wally Joyner, their first baseman, was struggling, so they made the trade for me, since I could play both positions. Karri and I packed up and made the move cross-country to San Diego. After what the Red Sox had accused her of, she was glad to be leaving Boston. And I was okay with being back in California. San Diego was a true breath of fresh air—what a beautiful city. But all the trades—Yankees–Anaheim (1997), Anaheim–Texas (1997), Texas–Boston (1998), and Boston–San Diego (1998)—took a heavy toll on my family. By the time we landed in San Diego, Austin was four and Dakota was two. The constant wear and tear of travel during the baseball season—plus the switching of teams and all the moving—continued to chip away at the foundation of my marriage.

8

Stand and Deliver

My first game with the Padres was on the night of June 22, 1998 in Seattle. Padres' pitcher Sterling Hitchcock, a former Yankee, was the scheduled pitcher that night. After a few bad starts, he was facing the threat of a demotion to the bullpen, and this was his last chance to turn it all around. Talk about being on the defense. Padres' manager Bruce Bochy (a former

catcher) called me into his office before the game and
asked whether I was up to catching that night. I'd been
Hitchcock's personal catcher with the Yankees and we
had a winning record together. I hadn't been behind the
plate for a year, but I jumped at the opportunity to work
with Hitchcock again, especially when the stakes were so
high for him.

Sure enough, I was behind the plate that night. I had
two doubles and three RBIs. More important, we won
3–0. Hitchcock pitched a great game: six innings, two
hits, five strikeouts, and only one earned run. From that
night on, I was once again Hitchcock's personal catcher.
He had a terrific season—MVP in the National League
Championship Series (NLCS). I helped him get a nice
contract for the next few years.

Except for Hitchcock, I didn't know many of the other
Padres. I wasn't very vocal or outgoing in San Diego.
Even though I wasn't catching every day, I was at least
catching Hitchy every five days. I knew the Padres didn't
get me for the regular season; I believed that the Padres
obtained me for the postseason. They knew what I could
do in big games.

I had not played in the National League before, and
even though I was not the starting catcher, every day I
went to the ballpark, there was a chance to get into the
game. I could pinch-hit or play defense. I also had the
chance to play with another future Hall of Famer—

Tony Gwynn. Gwynn, then in his seventeenth year with the Padres, was headed to Cooperstown. I had already played with two of the other greatest hitters of this era: Don Mattingly and Wade Boggs. I was thrilled to be on the same field now with Tony. When I arrived, the Padres were in first place, and as the season progressed, I became more and more comfortable as a part of the team. Before the last game of the season in Arizona, all of the guys were sitting around the locker room watching the NFL football games and playing their guitars. About thirty minutes before game time, Tony came back into the locker room and yelled at all of the guys to get ready to play the game. He told the clubhouse attendant to turn off all of the TV's and screamed that he wanted twenty-five guys on the bench before the game started. He said that the Padres had a chance to go to the World Series this year, but that it would take all twenty-five guys on the team to get there. We all had to support one another. I thought he was joking until I noticed every one getting quiet and heading to their lockers to get dressed. Nobody stood up to Gwynn—not even veterans like Trevor Hoffman (our closer) or the short-tempered Kevin Brown. Nobody. He was a perennial .300 hitter and had been selected to thirteen All-Star teams, had five Gold Gloves for his outfield play, and had led the National League in batting eight times. He was the greatest Padre of all time. But I'd been to the play-offs and had won a World Series, so I felt that I had a right to speak up. I told Gwynn that he had not been a leader all season long, so what was the deal now? "You want twenty-five guys on the field? Fine. But when *you're* taken out of a game in the sixth inning for a defensive replacement—whether it's me, Rivera, or somebody else—you better sit down and support them." Once removed from a game, Gwynn usually went into the clubhouse and stayed there. "You want twenty-five guys on the bench supporting you? You want to be a leader? I agree with you. I like that. But you have to back it up."

Sure enough, Gwynn was lifted for a pinch-hitter in the sixth inning. I was standing by the tunnel, waiting to see if Gwynn would go into the clubhouse. He didn't. Then Bochy put me in to pinch-hit in the seventh. I hit a ground ball right back to the pitcher for an out. As I came back to the dugout, pitcher Andy Ashby said to me, "Jimmy, your boy is in the locker room."

I ran right into the locker room, followed by Ashby and Kevin Brown. There was Gwynn in a Windbreaker and shorts, with a snack bowl in his hand. I said, "What the hell are you doing? Are you kidding me? Weren't you the one who just gave the speech about twenty-five guys, and 'Let's get ready for the play-offs,' and now you're in here eating instead of on the bench supporting your teammates?"

Gwynn said, "I didn't take myself out of the game. Bochy did."

I replied, "That's right. Bochy did. Not me, not Rivera, not the guys in your dugout. You better get on the field, or I'll carry you out in front of all these guys. You gave the speech, now back it up." Some of the guys in the clubhouse who heard my ranting said, "He's not coming down." I said, "You watch." Mid-inning, Gwynn came back into the dugout. He sat on the bench in uniform and taped his bats.

The next day we went to Houston to play the Astros. During pregame workouts, I walked over to Tony in the outfield. "I didn't mean to show you up," I said apologetically. "I played with Don Mattingly and Wade Boggs. I like your attitude, but I don't like fake people. You didn't back it up. I know who you are. I know that you are one of the greatest Padres of all time. I respect you as a hitter and what you've done for this team. But that stops right here. I know what it takes to win. I've been a winner all my life. And I proved that in 1996." Tony acknowledged that I hadn't shown him up but he still wasn't happy that I challenged him in front of the entire team.

I didn't worry that he might think I was out of line or making mountains out of molehills. Team morale and practicing what you preach have always been important to me and both were being jeopardized, as were our chances to make the play-offs. To win, you need to be unified and not distracted by pettiness and ego—even from Tony Gwynn. I wanted to nip any instances of these in the bud

before we got to the postseason. But I didn't care. That's
the way I was. As my teammate Trevor Hoffman said,
"Sometimes Jimmy told people what they didn't want to
hear. He was straight up." But every night when I put my
head on my pillow, I felt at ease. I spoke my mind and was
confident about my decision to do so. If you're going to
talk the talk, you better walk the walk. That's how I am
and that's what I expect from others.

The next day in Houston, during our workout day,
I was in the outfield. My teammates, Trevor Hoffman,
Andy Ashby, and Mark Sweeney were teasing me. They
said, "Dude, you're out of here. No way are you coming
back. People just don't talk that way to Tony Gwynn."
Apparently, nobody had ever spoken to Tony Gwynn—
now a Hall of Famer—like that before. But I didn't think
I'd done anything wrong.

Going into the play-offs in 1998, I didn't know exactly
what my role was going to be because we weren't sure
who we were going to face. Once we learned it would be
the Houston Astros, I knew they had at least three lefties
in their rotation who I would definitely face. The Astros'
closer was Billy Wagner, against whom I might be called
upon to pinch-hit against in the late innings. I was really
looking forward to the National League Division Series
that year.

I had a good play-off run with the Padres and helped
propel them to the National League postseason. Once we

got there, my bat got hot and I began doing what I do in the postseason: hitting clutch home runs. I started Game 1 in Houston at first base. I faced Randy Johnson, with whom I had a history, and singled in the second inning. In the sixth, I just missed a home run to center field and had to settle for a sacrifice fly that drove in Tony Gwynn to give us a 1–0 lead. Greg Vaughn homered in the eighth inning to secure the 2–0 victory for the Padres.

I didn't start the second game. We were down 4–2 with the Padres coming to bat in the ninth inning. The Astros brought in reliever Billy Wagner. I was sent in to pinch-hit for Wally Joyner with Ken Caminiti on first. After seeing about nine pitches, I homered to tie the game at 4, then stayed in to play first base. We still had the opportunity to win the game. Even though the Astros eked out a 5–4 victory, my two-run home run in the ninth started to shift the momentum of the series. My homer had put doubt into Billy Wagner's mind.

I started Game 3 catching Kevin Brown in front of 65,000 fans at home in San Diego. The Astros' starter was lefty Mike Hampton, followed in the seventh by Scott Elarton. In the bottom of the seventh, the game was tied at 1. I thought that Padres' manager Bruce Bochy might pinch-hit for me, but he didn't, and I homered to give the Padres a 2–1 victory. Now we were up 2–1 in the best of five series.

Sterling Hitchcock started Game 4 for the Padres, and I led off the second inning of Game 4 with a home run off Randy Johnson. Getting an early lead off a great pitcher like Johnson was important in the postseason, where most games were low-scoring. This home run gave us confidence that we could hit him.

This was my third home run in four days in the National League Division Series, and it made me feel great. Everybody on the Padres was surprised. We beat the Astros 6–1 and took the series 3–1 over the heavily favored Astros. Next, we faced the Atlanta Braves in the National League Championship Series, with the winner to play in the World Series. On October 11, I hit another key home run off Denny Neagle in the sixth inning of Game 5 of the NLCS against the Braves to put San Diego ahead in the seventh inning. We wound up losing that game 8–3, but we won the series 4–2 in Atlanta and celebrated big time! For the first time in franchise history, the Padres would be in the World Series, and we'd play my old team: the New York Yankees!

The glory was stripped from us against the Yanks in the 1998 World Series, but not without some ceremony. It was my second appearance in a World Series in three years and in the same stadium, but in different dugouts. It was Tony Gwynn's first World Series and first trip to Yankee Stadium, so experiencing that with him gave a lot of meaning to the Series, despite my going 0 for 10 and our being swept by the Yankees. And just like that, the season was over.

— ~

By 1999 I was a veteran. I had played in three post-
seasons and two World Series, something most players
just dream about. The 1999 season began with a phone
call from my agent asking if I wanted to return to San
Diego. I said yes, but I wanted management and the team
to know that I was going to be even more vocal—more of
a leader. If similar things happened with Gwynn or with
others, I was going to call them out. Despite my run-in
with Gwynn, I really liked him and the young team. I'd
been rather quiet (at least for me) during the 1998 season,
but I did speak up when I thought it was warranted. The
team was already established by the time I got there, and
I just tried to fit in. I knew I was there to help get through
the season, but they really got me for the postseason. The
year 1999 would be different.

Things went well at the start of the season. On June
21, we played the Dodgers in Los Angeles. Chan Ho Park
drilled me with a pitch and broke my left hand. I was
devastated. I was having a good year, and knew I might
be traded soon to a team that was going to the play-offs.
By this time, I was kind of a rent-a-player. Teams would
pick me up at the end of the year if they were going to
the postseason because of my previous success in the
play-offs. I just didn't know where I might go, and with a

broken hand didn't know if I would be ready by July 31. By now the Padres were rebuilding for the future. They were out of the race.

I worked out very hard. I stayed with the team throughout my rehab to show my support for the guys who were actually playing. (Most players on the disabled list stay home with their families and wait until they are close to returning before rejoining the team. This is especially true when the team is on the road. Players on the disabled list don't usually travel because it costs the team extra expenses.) I threw batting practice, but swinging a bat was still very painful. I was healing faster than I'd expected. I continued to work out and to stay in shape until July 20, still not knowing my fate.

I was rehabbing my left hand, trying to show that I would be healthy enough to swing a bat. I was sent to the Padres Rookie League team, the Quakes, in Rancho Cucamonga to get into some games. I had seven or eight at bats, but I was afraid that I was going to get hit because pitchers at this level do not have very good control. So I was sent to the Las Vegas Stars, the Padres' AAA team in the very competitive Pacific Coast League to face better pitching. By my third day in Las Vegas, Padres' general manager Kevin Towers called to tell me that there was a possibility of my being traded to the Boston Red Sox. Carlos Hernandez had become the Padres' regular catcher. I told Kevin and my agents that although I wanted to be traded somewhere where I could play every day, and traded to a play-off-bound team, Boston was *not* my first choice because Joe Kerrigan was still there.

I called Debbie Nicolosi, Mr. Steinbrenner's assistant at the Yankees. I asked her to tell Steinbrenner, general manager Brian Cashman, and anybody else who'd listen that the Padres were about to trade me to Boston. I would much rather be back in New York. My experience in Boston left a sour taste in my mouth.

If my call had been revealed at the time, I could have been charged with tampering. League rules don't allow that while a player is still under contract. I just didn't think the Yankees wanted me to go to the Boston Red Sox. On July 31, 1999, the Padres traded me back to my old team, the New York Yankees, for Geraldo Padua, a career minor leaguer. I was going home.

9

You Can Never Go Home

Ijumped at the chance to go back to the Yankees. The
New York headlines shouted that I was coming back
to help them, though I can't say that was the main reason
for my return. Perhaps it was simply to keep me from the
Red Sox, the Yankees' main rival in the American League
East.

When I arrived in New York, I was bombarded by

questions from local sportswriters about returning. Why was I here? I answered that I was glad to be back, and that I was looking forward to performing in the postseason. That's exactly the way I felt, but frankly, with my broken left hand, I didn't know what I was capable of. I walked into Joe Torre's office. He told me that Steinbrenner had wanted me, but that he (Torre) had not—nice to be told that my new manager didn't want me on the team.

Torre told me that I wasn't back to catch Pettitte. The Yankees already had two excellent catchers: Jorge Posada and Joe Girardi. They didn't need me behind the plate. I was going to pinch-hit for lefties and occasionally spell Tino Martinez at first base. I said, "No problem." I was just glad to be out of San Diego, where they'd conducted a fire sale, trading or selling their veterans after making the World Series. I told the reporters that I'd help the team any way I could to win a championship. This sounds like a cliché, but it was true. I just wanted to play.

I didn't have full strength in my left hand yet. Derek Jeter, Chuck Knoblauch, Tino Martinez, and others all made good fun of me because it was so hard for me to swing a bat with a broken wrist, even in batting practice. My left hand was still in a brace, and I knew I couldn't hit a home run if my life depended on it. I told them that I'd recover soon enough. Then I boldly predicted, "When I hit a home run, it will be an important one!"

I only got into thirty-nine games the rest of the season

and didn't homer, and therefore can't take any credit for the Yankees becoming the American League champions in 1999. After beating the Texas Rangers and the Boston Red Sox in the postseason, we were back in the World Series, my third in four years.

In Game 1 in Atlanta, I pinch-hit for outfielder Ricky Ledee to face the hard-throwing reliever John Rocker in the top of the eighth. The Yankees were ahead 3–1. Derek Jeter was on third, Paul O'Neill on second, and Bernie Williams on first. I walked, driving in Jeter, making the score. Yankees 4, Braves 1.

In Game 4, with the Yankees ahead 3–1, Terry Mulholland came in to relieve John Smoltz in the bottom of the eighth inning. Bernie Williams popped to second, and Tino Martinez fouled out to the catcher. With two outs, I pinch-hit for Darryl Strawberry, the DH. As I came to the plate, I thought this may be my last at bat of the 1999 season—the last of the twentieth century. I worked the count full. Then Mulholland came in with a fastball. I swung away and connected. The ball went toward the 399-foot sign in left center. Bob Costas, broadcasting the game, said, "Did he do it again? Yes!" As I rounded the bases, Costas said, "You can send this guy to a resort all summer, as long as you bring him back for October."

I returned to the dugout fired up. I think we all remembered that I had predicted that I would eventually hit an important home run. A euphoric Paul O'Neill asked,

"Are you kidding me? Can you believe it?" I couldn't believe it myself. With the Yankees on top 4–1 in the game, and ahead 3–0 in the Series, unless the Braves came back in the top of the ninth, the Yankees would not bat again. My wife later told me that her father said, "Do you realize that that was the last home run of the twentieth century?" The Braves never recovered, and the Yankees swept them 4–0.

Although I hadn't contributed much to the Yankees' success in 1999, that home run made me feel like a part of the team. Not since Yogi Berra in 1947—more than a half century before—had a Yankee hit a pinch-hit home run in the World Series.

~ ~

During the off-season in 1999, my hand healed, but my left shoulder began to bother me. An MRI disclosed that I had a slight tear in the left rotator cuff. I had the surgery right away and five weeks later was ready for spring training in 2000.

As spring training approached, Steinbrenner called my agent and offered me a two-year contract for a million dollars per year. That was a lot of money for me. In 1990, my first season with the Yankees, I made $100,000. In 1991, that was raised to $135,000. By 1992, it was cut to $126,500. I got a raise in 1993 to $152,000, and a big raise in 1994: $742,500. I nearly doubled that in 1995, when I earned $1,350,000—my first million-dollar-plus contract—with another raise in 1996 to $1,470,000. In 1997, the Angels paid me $1,916,972, but the most I ever made was with the Boston Red Sox: 2 million dollars (more than $38,000 per week). In 1999, the Padres cut that to $1,900,000, and in 2000, my final year in the majors, I turned down the Yankees' offer of a million a year for two years, settling instead for a one-year contract for only one million.

I asked my agents how many at bats I was likely to get. At that time, I was slated to be the right-handed DH. Darryl Strawberry was going to be the left-handed DH. When I heard that, I signed, but only for *one* year. I thought that if I had 300–400 at bats, I'd have a good year and be in a position to demand $5 million to $6 million for 2001.

But things change, especially in baseball. On January 19, 2000, Strawberry failed his third drug test. On February 28, he was suspended from baseball for a year. Shortly thereafter, Steinbrenner called my agent to ask, "Can your boy handle the full-time DH duties?" My agent said, "Yes!" I thought, *What a great opportunity. I'll get my 500–600 at bats as an everyday player, a chance to put up big numbers, and make a lot of money.*

I was very excited in spring training. I concentrated on running and hitting, knowing that finally, I'd play full-time. The Yankees had a regular catcher in Jorge Posada, and they signed Tom Pagnozzi from St. Louis as Posada's backup. Chris Turner was also signed as a third backup catcher, but not on the forty-man roster, which means that if the Yankees kept him, they'd have to take another player off the roster. They didn't want to do that for a backup catcher. (By this time, Joe Girardi was gone; he'd signed with the Chicago Cubs as a free agent.)

Torre told me that I'd be the regular, full-time DH—not the backup catcher. That was fine with me. But then, with just two weeks left in spring training, Pagnozzi blew out his shoulder, and his career was over. Torre told me that I would still get my at bats, but I would also be the backup catcher: rookie Shane Spencer would be the DH.

I had a feeling that this was the writing on the wall. I didn't play because I was the backup catcher. If Posada got hurt, I'd have to catch. If I had been in the game as the DH and went in to catch, we'd lose the DH and the pitcher would have to bat. Nobody wanted that.

As the season started, we'd already faced four or five left-handed pitchers I still hadn't played. So I walked into Joe Torre's office to complain. I told him that I'd been promised that I'd play full-time, which was why I'd only signed a one-year contract. I wanted to know what was going on. The Yankees had told me that this was going to be my year, my opportunity. Had I known it was going to be like this, I would have taken the extra million dollars and signed for two years. He offered no real explanation and the situation continued to get worse and worse—more left-handed pitchers and still no playing time.

By June, I had appeared in only twenty-four games and had only fifty-five at bats. I was very unhappy. In fact, I was miserable—both on and off the field. My marriage to Karri was falling apart again, and now my career looked like it would end after 2000—unless, of course, I could get an at bat in the postseason and do something special again. Maybe then I could salvage another lost season.

Chuck Knoblauch suddenly developed a mental block and could no longer throw the ball from second base to first. The Yankees tried to let him play through it, but by June 20, they couldn't wait any longer. The Yankees pulled the trigger and traded me to the Los Angeles Dodgers for infielder José Vizcaíno. The Dodgers needed a right-handed bat off the bench to complement Dave Hansen, their left-handed pinch-hitter.

Unfortunately, the trade was made around 11:00 PM. We were in Boston, and my wife Karri and I were out with some of my teammates and their wives at a bar called Daisy's. David Cone and I were at the bar getting drinks. *SportsCenter* was on the TV set behind the bar. All of a sudden Coney said, "Dude, you just got traded to the Dodgers!" Of course, we laughed—we thought it was a joke. But no, it was true: the ticker at the bottom of the TV screen said that Jim Leyritz had just been traded by the Yankees to the Dodgers for José Vizcaíno.

When Karri and I got back to the hotel, there was a message for me. Brian Cashman had called. He needed to speak with me as soon as possible. Just like that, my dream of retiring as a Yankee ended. Karri had just found out she was pregnant again and this sent her over the edge. She blamed me and decided to go home to Fort Lauderdale instead of accompanying me to L.A. She had morning sickness, and trying to take care of the two boys was just too much for her. She was no longer willing to pick up and move to another home 3,000 miles away. I was devastated. I begged God for guidance and wondered if this was a sign that I should give up baseball entirely.

Being a major-league baseball player is not as glamorous as you might think. There is a lot of uncertainty: moving around, being treated like the commodity that I was, and having to learn to relinquish my power and "plans" to the ups and downs of the game. You do get paid *very* well. People recognize you. Your face is on baseball cards and in the newspapers. Fans ask for your autograph. You eat at nice restaurants and stay in deluxe hotels. And if you're single, all that can be a lot of fun. But there is a downside, too: mainly the travel. First, there's the wear and tear on your body from the hotel to the bus to the airport to the bus to the ballpark—then the same routine all over again. If you're coming off an injury, it can be even more grueling. It's also very hard on your family life.

I had learned from my first marriage that to stay faithful and happily married, you had to take your wife and family on most of your road trips. You had to avoid the loneliness and separation and keep your family as close to you as possible.

But to do that also requires tremendous sacrifices. Many ballplayers miss watching their children grow up. They miss dance or music recitals, birthday parties, the school plays, meeting their friends and their friends' parents, the class trips, the big games, or just helping the kids with their homework. I wanted to watch my young sons grow up, so during my big-league career, I took my wife and children on every road trip. We had a nanny to accompany us so Karri and I could go out occasionally and be alone together. It wasn't unusual for us to run into married players who were with women on the road other than their wives. This caused some tension with many of my teammates. They'd get mad and say, "What are you doing with your wife in the hotel lobby (or at the bar)?"

My attitude was, "This is who I am. I'm with my wife. If you don't like it, don't cheat on your wife, or at least keep it in your room." I used to be one of those players, but I wasn't anymore. I wanted my wife and kids with me. But it was expensive.

In order to join me, Karri and the boys had to fly separately on commercial flights, and we would always have to get an extra room at the team hotel for the nanny and the boys. I used to spend between $30,000 and $40,000 each year just to have my family travel with me. But I felt it was important to stick together. I had lost one marriage to being apart and I was now losing another marriage because of the toll it took to stay together.

I never missed the boys' first steps or first words and I got to be there for the important moments and milestones in their lives. We were home together or they were with me on the road. A very difficult way for a family to live. But a far cry from the partying and crazy lifestyle that some people believe I led. Don't get me wrong: Karri and I went out and occasionally drank, mostly because we didn't like staying home with each other. But we also got to wake up with the boys in the morning and spend the day together until I had to play a game every night.

Don Mattingly and Wade Boggs once gave me invaluable advice. They told me to keep my family close, because they said when I left baseball, unless I lived in the same town or raised my kids together with a teammate, I wasn't going to have many friends from my baseball days. Once you leave the game, your family is all you have. They also told me that when they got home and their kids were thirteen or fourteen years old, it was tough because their children were already in routines that didn't include them. It was almost like you were interrupting the life that they were used to without you around. I didn't want that for me. It is no accident that things happened the way they did. God knew it would keep me very close to my children, and my children close to me, which has come to be my saving grace and the only thing that has kept me going during the events that would later transpire in my life.

I flew to Los Angeles to finish the season by myself. We both hoped this new baby would save our marriage, and for a short time it did. I was so excited to be having another boy. But now living in two different cities, I just wasn't sure.

The Dodgers slowly fell out of the play-off picture, and then I injured myself while playing the outfield for Gary Sheffield when I ran into a wall and separated my right shoulder. On September 15, I played my last game as a Dodger and went home to have surgery. This ended my 2000 season. I started my rehab right away.

———

At thirty-six, I wasn't ready to retire. That's when I started taking human growth hormone (HGH). I thought it would help me heal faster. I had no contract, so I needed to show that I was healthy enough to play. I was willing to return as a spring training non-roster invitee or as a minor leaguer. The Mets invited me to spring training. *Great*! I thought. Their spring training camp is in Port St. Lucie, Florida, about an hour from our home, so if Karri went into labor, I could get back in time. Sure enough, on February 27, 2001, Phoenix Casey Leyritz entered the world in Fort Lauderdale. I was there for his birth. What a thrill! He was healthy and things looked good—for him, for Karri, and for me.

My agents told the Mets that I wasn't going to be ready by March 30, so I might have to start the year at AAA, the top minor-league level. I asked for a guaranteed contract of at least $500,000. The Mets agreed, but they failed to inform manager Bobby Valentine about my shoulder injury. So when I arrived at the Mets camp on February 15, 2001, Valentine told me to go catch. I told him, "Hey, I'm not ready yet. I'm still rehabbing my shoulder." He was visibly surprised and not very happy. In a game toward the end of spring training, Valentine put me in at third base. I hurt my right shoulder again. The Mets called me in on March 17 and told me that they couldn't wait for me to be healthy. They released me.

10

Family First

A s much as I was frustrated about being released from the Mets (I was only two or three weeks away from being back in playing shape and I knew I could still play), it led me back home to Fort Lauderdale where I needed to be. I continued to work out and tried to stay in shape, waiting for a call.

In the meantime, I was able to be there with Phoenix

and his older brothers, and I didn't feel like going back to the minor leagues and trying to hang on. I also needed to see if Karri and I could salvage our marriage. After being home for just a short time, I realized that Karri and I still had big issues. As I look back on it now, this may have been God's way of telling me that it was time to go home, be a full-time dad, and give up the chance for one last good-bye tour in the bigs.

———

A few weeks later I got a call, but not the one I'd hoped for. It was from the Newark Bears in the independent Atlantic League. Tom Cetnar, the team's general manager (and now the team's owner) suggested that I come to Newark to play. This way, Cetnar said, thirty major-league teams would have a chance to see me instead of just one. At the time, both José Canseco and his identical twin brother Ozzie were playing there, as were Lance Johnson and Alonzo Powell—all former major leaguers.

It was a tough decision. I talked it over with Karri, and she agreed that I should sign. By that time, she wanted me gone anyway. With a nanny/housekeeper and her parents nearby, she didn't need me around. Plus, when I was home all we did was fight. Even though it was not for much money (only $3,000 per month), I decided to do it. I thought the visibility would be good for my future—it could help get me back to the majors.

In May, I went to play for Newark, which, unlike some other gambles I made in my career, turned out to be good decision. When I called home every day to check on the boys, Karri told me that everything was fine. Austin and Dakota were enrolled in the Flamingo Road Christian School, and she could spend the whole day with Phoenix. Karri told me to play hard and work myself back into shape to get back to the major leagues.

After just twenty-six days with the Bears, I got a contract to play for the San Diego Padres again. I was elated. This is what I had been working for. The Padres sent me to the Beavers, their AAA affiliate in Portland, Oregon, in the Pacific Coast League. They told me to play there for about ten days to get back into shape. I was told that when a spot opened up on the Padres' roster, they'd bring me up, perhaps by the end of June.

One night, the Beavers were getting killed by the Sky Sox in Colorado Springs. Sean Burroughs, the Padres' top prospect at third base, asked manager Rick Sweet to take him out of the game, saying, "I don't want to play anymore. I'm tired. I'm coming out of the lineup." The manager said, "Leyritz, pinch-hit for Burroughs." I tried to play the veteran's card and said, "I'm too important to pinch-hit for Sean," but it didn't work, and I went up to pinch-hit in a blowout game. The third pitch I saw was a fastball inside that hit me directly on the right wrist, breaking my hand.

Predictably, Karri didn't seem too happy to learn that I was on my way home. Our marriage wasn't any better, and the distance made it easier to ignore. After recuperating for eight weeks, we were both ready for me to go back to work. When I arrived in Portland, I homered in four straight games and felt ready to get back to the big leagues. But in the next game, I took a swing and pulled my entire stomach muscle. I had to be helped up and off the field. I stayed in the team hotel for two days and had to sleep in a chair. I was in excruciating pain. Damn. I was so close to getting back to the majors. I was only thirty-eight—and I wanted to keep going.

It was during this time that Karri noticed that our youngest son Phoenix, then four months old, had a flat shape to the back of his head. She took him to the doctor who sent us to a specialist who diagnosed Phoenix with craniosynostosis, the same disease that Jorge Posada's young son, Jorge Jr., had. Craniosynostosis is a very rare disease affecting about .005 percent of the population (1 in 2,000). The plates of the baby's skull close prematurely and therefore do not allow room for proper brain growth. Sure enough, Phoenix had a fusion of two bones in the back of his head, which was responsible for the deformity in its shape. Unless the plates were separated surgically,

Phoenix's brain would not grow and fully develop. The doctor told us that Phoenix would need this surgery before he turned nine months old. The doctor explained to us that he did not feel this was a major surgery, but to us it was terrifying.

About a week before the surgery I was changing Phoenix on the bed. I turned around to get a diaper, and he pushed himself off the bed. He fell on the floor and got a big bump on his head. The bump got bigger so Karri and I took him to the emergency room. The hematoma continued to grow. We finally found out that the reason the bump kept growing is that Phoenix was also Factor XI (FXI) deficient: he had hemophilia C. Even a severe bruise could be very dangerous for him. We were stunned. They treated him with plasma and whole blood and his condition improved. But his surgery had to be postponed in order to get more plasma and whole blood ready for him.

He finally had the surgery in October 2001 at the Joe DiMaggio Hospital in Hollywood, Florida, and everything went relatively well. Still, Phoenix was in pain due to having half of his skull removed and replaced with titanium, and Karri was struggling with anxiety as she tried to deal with him being in pain. A doctor prescribed Xanax for her. It was good that I was home at this time to help with the two older boys. The stress was really beginning to take its toll on Karri.

We later found out another example of how miraculously God works. If the craniosynostosis operation had proceeded before the hemophilia diagnosis, we would have lost him during the surgery since his bleeding would have been uncontrolled and enough lifesaving plasma and blood would not have been prepared. Phoenix could have bled to death. When Phoenix turned five, he no longer needed regular treatment for his hemophilia; his condition is now under control.

Phoenix had fully recovered from his surgery, although he was required to wear a special helmet to shape his head correctly for the entire next year. Shortly after that, the Mayagüez Indians offered me $10,000 per month to play ball in the Puerto Rico Winter League. I didn't have a job and I needed to earn some money. I couldn't turn it down. I went and played there for a month.

I came home from Puerto Rico to attend my best friend's wedding, which we were hosting at our house. Karri wasn't in great shape. She had lost a lot of weight and seemed distant but she assured me that she was doing okay and that she and the boys were alright. I left for Puerto Rico to finish the season and play-offs. I was only home for a brief time and I had to turn around and go back in two days. I had to return at this time because this is when the teams sent down all their scouts to see if players were ready for the spring.

About a week later, our housekeeper called me in

Puerto Rico. She said that when she arrived for work in the morning, Karri was passed out in bed and wouldn't wake up. Austin (six) and Dakota (four) were by the pond in front of our house playing without any supervision. Phoenix was lying in his crib in a filthy diaper. At the time, the doctors who prescribed the Xanax for Karri didn't realize that she was a former abuser. Neither did I. I was on the next flight home.

When I walked in the door, I found Karri in bed and her godmother, Joy, sitting nearby. Joy proceeded to tell me that she was going to take Karri to the hospital to detox. Apparently, her entire family knew she had battled drug addiction as a teenager and no one bothered to tell me. I was shocked and furious. The previous couple of off-seasons we had begun living a rock-and-roll lifestyle: lots of parties and late nights. But very rarely were any drugs involved, especially prescription drugs. Her mother tried to convince me to give her another chance—that this wasn't who she *really* was—the drugs were responsible for her behavior. What was I to do? I had three young children and this was their mother. Who would take care of them?

With Karri in the hospital, some of my friends began to tell me what had been going on in my absence. One of them asked me if I had heard about what happened to our Jeep. I responded, "Yes, Karri claimed that someone had broken into our garage and stolen it." The friend advised me to go talk to the owner of the country bar we always hung out in to find out what really happened. I knew the owner and went straight to the bar. Sure enough, he told me that she had been coming in a lot. She had told him that we were separated and she was running around with an eighteen-year-old kid. He had to finally kick them out because he found out the kid was underage. He also told me a story about the night that she lost our Jeep. This took me by surprise, but I played along with him as if I knew what he was talking about. The bar owner told me that she was so wasted that she gave some stranger the keys, thinking he was a friend of this kid she was with, but he wasn't. This person took off with the Jeep and it was never seen again.

I also found out she had been leaving our children with the nanny and her parents for extended periods of time so she could stay out. The boys were still too young to know much, but they did say enough to convince me that Mommy had been sleeping all day and was out all night. They also said that some guys were coming to the house for cookouts. In desperation, I researched as much as I could and talked to several different counselors about addiction, something I knew nothing about. They all convinced me that if Karri could get off the drugs, our family had a shot. I looked to God for answers and decided to forgive Karri—I wanted to keep our family in tact. She entered a brief treatment facility and returned home in January 2002.

That month, when I was trying to come back, there were not many friends I could turn to for help in opening a door. I called some of my former coaches and managers without much success. I started to see that what Mattingly and Boggs had told me was true: Once you leave the game for a while, people forget you. Loyalty was only as good as your last hit. Unfortunately, it had been a few years since I'd ended the season with a dramatic postseason home run. The adage, "What have you done for me lately?" was never more true.

In February, I received an invitation to the Yankees' spring training. By now we had almost no money. We had bought our dream house in Fort Lauderdale thinking I would play for at least five more years but then I got hurt. I was really feeling the pressure to find steady work. I decided to take the Yankees' invitation and see if I could make it. But my shoulder wasn't ready and the Yankees released me at the end of March, so I came home. Karri and I were living in the same house but were rarely together and were basically just there for the kids. The bills were piling up and I needed to find something.

❦

I hadn't worked since the Yankees released me in 2002. In 2003, the Mexican summer league offered me $12,000 a month to play in Oaxaca. Karri seemed better at the time and told me to go. I was reluctant to leave the boys again but I didn't have a choice—I had to provide for my family. I left Karri and the kids at home and went to play for the Oaxaca Guerreros in the Mexican League. Although I was only there three weeks, I was doing well and I hit a grand slam in my ninth or tenth game. Several major-league scouts were watching, which I took as a good sign. We'd lost our left fielder, and I wanted to show off for the scouts— not hot dogging, but just to show that I could still play the outfield too. Chasing a fly ball into our bull pen, I stepped into a drainage hole that was left open. That last step would be my last ever as a player on a baseball field. My ankle snapped and I knew it was broken. Again, I had to call Karri and tell her I was done, but this time I was *really* done. I took the next flight home. No more comebacks, no more baseball.

When I returned home, Karri was again having problems and was neglecting our sons. My children were being taken care of by our nanny, Magdalena, and not by their mother. Karri had gone on another binge, repeating what we'd gone through the year before: partying and drinking heavily. She was using pills again and running around town. I thank God Magdalena was there to look after the boys and protect them. She cared for them deeply and I will always be grateful for her. Had something tragic happened to the boys in my absence I would have never forgiven myself.

The boys were getting old enough to realize something was wrong, and I could not live this way any longer. Mom and Dad weren't loving toward each other, and Karri wanted to continue the lifestyle that I no longer wanted to be a part of. Karri and I entered counseling as a last resort. The problem was, she didn't want to be honest with the counselor about everything that was happening. We would go to counseling and talk about our surface problems and the changes we needed to make, but once we left the office, we would go out and drink together and sweep the main issues back under the rug. I knew it would never work. The boys were then seven, five, and two and needed a stable and wholesome home life. The days of going out to clubs and staying out all night were over. It was time to surround myself with responsible people and make the kids, rather than my own personal life, a priority.

With a heavy heart, I asked Karri to move out. No more chances: I wanted a divorce. I offered to get her an apartment and told her that this marriage and the lifestyle we had been leading were over. I filed for divorce the next day. I began going back to church, and I asked God for forgiveness for some of the poor decisions that I had made that contributed to the demise of my family. I couldn't believe I was going to go through another divorce. I felt like a failure.

Once my ankle healed, the Padres and others offered me minor-league contracts for 2004, if I was healthy enough. If I made the big-league team, I'd get $500,000.

If not, $175,000 to play in the minors. I called my father and explained everything that was going on. I said there were a few teams that wanted me to come back and play, but it would mean I would have to leave the boys with Karri and she was still unstable. My father already felt like Karri had ruined my career, so this was a hard call to make. My dad told me, "Jimmy, *you* have to decide. I can't do it for you. But God will give you the answer if you pray on it." I prayed harder that night than I think I ever had before and woke up the next morning with the answer: give up baseball. It was time to come home and be the best teammate of all—Dad. I decided to "hang up my spikes" and become a full-time father. I felt my kids had no chance without me, and somehow I would figure out a way to make ends meet. I called my dad back to tell him of my decision. He told me that as much as he was proud of me for what I had accomplished on the field, he was most proud of me for putting my family first. I hung up with tears in my eyes and began to do some serious soul searching. It was time to stop jumping in and out of my faith. I had to commit completely to a new life where God was the number one priority.

In my eleven-year major-league career, I had more than 300 at bats only twice: in 1990, my rookie season with the Yankees (303), and in 1997, which I split between the Anaheim Angels and the Texas Rangers (379). I think this is why it was so hard for me to consider retirement. Even with all of my injuries, trades, playing in the minors, in the independent league, and even in Puerto Rico and Mexico, leaving baseball meant I was going to have to face real life. By myself, alone, with only my boys. In retrospect, the timing of my last injury could not have been better. Breaking my ankle sent me home to my boys when they needed me most. And I finally got it: God had been calling me home over and over because my boys needed me. This time, I got the message.

11

Happy Birthday

Once I filed for divorce, Karri accused me of abusing her and the boys. Her attorney filed restraining
orders against me. Our great judicial system sometimes seems to assume that we're guilty *before* proven
innocent, especially in divorce cases where the mother
usually gets the benefit of the doubt. I was forced to
spend thousands of dollars and countless hours with the

Department of Child Welfare before all of Karri's allegations were proven false. Once the judge dropped all
the restraining orders, I began to fight for full custody
of the boys for two reasons: First, I wanted to be their
full-time father; I knew it was a job I was ready to do.
Second, I knew that Karri couldn't take care of them
any longer and I didn't want the boys exposed to the
lifestyle she continued to live. The drawn-out court pro-
ceedings took a lot out of me, physically and emotionally. I didn't particularly like discussing our personal life
with lawyers and in court. I wanted to keep all of our
dirty laundry out of the papers and keep things private.
And, of course, this was all very draining financially. I
spent about $450,000 on lawyers' fees, since I paid for
Karri's lawyers as well as mine.

The custody battle and impending divorce became
more than contentious. I was in New York for an appearance when I got a phone call informing me that Karri
and some friends had brought a few vans to my home to
remove all of my belongings from the house. I called the
police to ask them to get over there. The police told me
that unfortunately, they couldn't intervene because legally
she was still my wife and the house was jointly owned. I
tried to explain that she'd moved out a month earlier, but
it didn't matter.

I returned home the next day to an empty house. Karri
had sold all of my baseball memorabilia including my

beloved World Series rings. And this was only the beginning of her true colors coming out. She actually sold the rings for less than a thousand dollars. (Aside from their sentimental value, which made them priceless, they were worth about $30,000 each. I couldn't live with the fact that the 1996 ring, especially, was gone, so I had a duplicate made as a consolation.) But she was on one of her binges again and needed to make a quick sale on whatever she could take from me.

Finally, I had my attorney file papers to have Karri drug-tested and psychologically evaluated. Sure enough, she tested positive for drugs and was diagnosed as bipolar. She was put on medication and was ordered to seek professional help. But after about three weeks, she stopped the treatment and therapy.

My divorce from Karri became final in July 2004, but the custody of Austin, Dakota, and Phoenix—my favorite team—was still unresolved. Although I'd earned about $11,000,000 during my eleven-year big-league baseball career, I spent almost all of it fighting for custody of my three sons and the expenses that go with a nasty divorce. I paid for the five lawyers that my ex-wife hired. She fired each one every time they discovered that she had no proof to back up the allegations she was trying to use against me. We started the divorce with $680,000 in an escrow account. By the time the divorce became final, we were left with just $12,000.

⌐ ～ ⌐

But it was worth it. I won primary custody of our sons and began to rebuild my life. In 2004, Major League Baseball.com (MLB.com) asked me to do a radio show for two hours a day. It started off Monday, Wednesday, and Friday, then progressed to five days a week. It was a show that I could do from my house and still be home to take care of the boys—the perfect setup for me at the time. I couldn't believe that I had been so blessed. Just one way maybe God was rewarding me for making that decision to come home and be a full-time father and to put my children's needs ahead of my own.

When we started, I was on from 11:00 AM to 1:00 PM. My broadcast partner in New York was Billy Sample, a former outfielder and designated hitter with the Rangers, Yankees, and Braves. We'd talk about the games and the moves various teams were making. We would also have five or six guests lined up each day to interview. I could be in my office working and be able to take care of the kids without any interruptions. MLB.com was a lifesaver. I loved what I was doing and began to have a lot of success with the show.

The first year I only made about $40,000 from my radio work, but the beauty of the show was that I could do the broadcast from home. This job permitted me to take the boys to school and to make sure that they were taken care of. But $40,000 is not enough to raise a family of four. Occasionally, I was able to fly to New York and do some autograph signings. I also did some meet-and-greet work for the Yankees, but they wanted me to do more. I needed to find a way to juggle the responsibilities of being a full-time father and still have the ability to travel more for work.

I had started a dating a young woman named Laura, who had a two-year-old son named Jagger. Laura's ex-husband wasn't paying child support, and she was in a bad situation. She was about to move out of her apartment, and my house had just been sold. The boys and I were renting an apartment of our own. I suggested that we move in together. It would be helpful to both of us. I could provide Jagger and her a roof over their heads and she could help me out with my children. She agreed and we moved in together the next month. At this time we still were dealing with a lot of issues pertaining to both of our exes. We knew it wouldn't be easy but we wanted the children to benefit from the security of a healthy relationship.

After our divorce, Karri began filing false accusations against me for every little thing. Her lawyer, *whom I was paying*, took advantage of her because he knew she had issues. She wouldn't get the kids to school on time, or she'd leave them there and forget to pick them up. The school would call and I'd have to go get them. Karri would come up with excuse after excuse as to why she wasn't a responsible parent. There were times when Laura and I were planning to go away for the weekend because the boys were supposed to be staying with Karri. Then Karri wouldn't pick them up and Laura and I would have to cancel our plans. This happened often and put tremendous stress on my relationship with Laura. We were a new couple trying to develop a bond with each other while also meeting the needs of four children.

Karri began filing false police reports to try to have me thrown in jail. She and I had restraining orders against each other. It was so ugly that Laura had the unfortunate role of being the go-between. We had social workers and guardians *ad litem*. Karri was not able to help take care of our three boys, so Laura and I were always on high alert when the boys were with Karri. Something always came up, whether it was her forgetting to pick the boys up from school or not showing up to make an exchange. Laura was put through hell with the constant problems Karri caused, but she loved the boys and did the best she could.

The Broward court system and Department of Children's Services wouldn't give me full custody of the boys. I tried time and time again. They told me that Karri wasn't physically abusing them and she had food in the refrigerator so the boys must be okay. The judge overseeing the divorce told me that although we had proven Karri was buying and selling prescription meds (even around the boys) and I felt she was emotionally and mentally abusing them, he didn't think they were in danger. He even commented that he couldn't do anything about "bad parenting." I was pissed. The system was a joke. I kept telling my attorney there was something that wasn't right about our judge's thought process. A year later I read in the paper that the same judge had been caught smoking pot during his lunch breaks and was removed from the bench. Unbelievable. These were the same people making critical decisions about the welfare of our children!

With Laura at home with the boys, I started making more money, and with the appearances during the summer for the Yankees, it was a very nice living. Despite all the problems with Karri, I asked Laura to marry me on Christmas Eve 2004 while we were out with some friends. She said yes and we agreed on a long engagement. Two years later I thought it was time to set a date and get serious about being married. I wanted the boys to have a stable family, and Laura was a great mother. Unfortunately, Karri's behavior got even worse, and it all became too much for Laura. She knew that if we married, it would never change, and she would always have to be cleaning up Karri's mess. She finally told me that she couldn't marry me. My relationship with Laura ended after three and a half years together. We remain friends to this day. My youngest son, Phoenix, and Laura's son, Jagger, have a special bond, almost like brothers. They still see each other at least once a month.

—◦—

Karri continued to intentionally cause me a lot of trouble. Her actions—not taking the boys to school, forgetting to pick them up when she did take them, trying to throw me in jail, and just plain hatred—were interfering with my efforts to give the boys the most stable, normal upbringing I could as a single parent trying to earn a living. Florida divorce laws were so weak; there was nothing I could do to stop her from interfering with my sons and me.

—◦—

In 2007, I got a job with ESPN radio. I went to every Yankee home game. I usually sat behind home plate with my former teammate Rich Monteleone, who charted pitches from that spot for the Yankees. He always had an extra seat next to him. After the game, I gave a two-minute report on the game for *Mike and Mike in the Morning*. On Fridays, I did a one-hour Yankee report on Michael Kay's radio show, dealing with the personalities on the team. As a former Yankee, I was able to provide stories and insights that other reporters didn't have. Once a month, I did a show with one of ESPN's reporters for a few hours, talking about the Yankees. They gave me a two-year deal at $100,000 per year. I enjoyed it. I was in New York for eighty-one days a year.

Through medication and therapy, Karri had stabilized enough that I felt comfortable leaving the boys in her care briefly while I was working. The courts wouldn't let me take the boys and move to New York, so I gave Karri a chance to see if she could help take care of them. Her parents still lived in Miami and were close enough if she needed help.

The boys (by this time ages twelve, ten, and six) seemed to be adjusting well to my being away for work—a stark contrast to 2004 when I could not leave them with Karri at all. Unfortunately, I was away for all of October 2007, covering the Yankees postseason, including their epic battle with the Boston Red Sox. Then I covered the entire World Series (Colorado Rockies versus the eventual winners, the Red Sox.)

When I returned home to Fort Lauderdale after the Series, I found out that Karri had not been taking the boys to school regularly. In fact, they were struggling in school and in almost everything else. So in November, I had a big decision to make. ESPN talked with me about increasing my role there. I knew I had to make a change that would let me be home more, or I had to fight to move the boys to New York with me. The Yankees made me a

very generous offer. They wanted me to do more suite
work, greeting VIPs and working on the field at their
summer youth instructional camps for underprivileged
kids during July and August. I filed the necessary paperwork to move the boys to New York with me. I would be
able to work full-time, knowing that they were safe and
being cared for. I had to wait for a judge to decide.

My broadcasting career was taking off. I had an opportunity to do some commercials for Bald Guyz, which
makes hair and scalp products for men who shave their
heads or are bald like me. We had planned a promotional
pool tournament. A real estate company in Lake Worth,
Florida, talked to me about being a spokesperson for a
firm that was going to develop 280 1.25-acre properties in
Costa Rica. This was my million-dollar deal.

Joya Pacifica wanted me to do their commercials for a
hefty sum. I was going to be the Eric Estrada of Costa
Rica. I would make 10 percent off every property that
I brought people in on, and 1.5 percent on every other
property sold through the infomercials that we had begun
to shoot. On top of that, they were also going to give me
two of the properties to build my own vacation home on.
This would be where I would retire to once the boys were
on their own.

Life was good and the future looked very bright—a
great gig and a great opportunity for me to make a lot
of money and secure my financial future. So many good

things were happening, and there were so many decisions
to make.

That November, while waiting for the custody hearing,
the boys and I began attending church regularly. I was
growing impatient and started questioning things. During Christmas Eve services in 2007, I asked God for help.
*Please tell me what to do. Give me a sign. Should I pursue
this career opportunity to make a lot of money and possibly
have to leave the boys home with their mother? Or should I
fight to take them with me to New York where I still would
be gone a lot? What should I do, Lord?* Three nights later,
God gave me the sign I had asked for. The way he deliv-
ered it was life shattering.

December 27, 2007—my forty-fourth birthday—began
as an ordinary day. The boys and I decided to spend the
day at the beach, where they could play and I could pick
up some belated Christmas presents at the mall. While
at the beach, Karri called and offered to take the boys
if I wanted to go out for my birthday. I hadn't made
any plans because most of my friends had to work the
next day. I decided to call my friend Robin and ended up
making plans to meet her and her boyfriend Mark for a
drink. She told me that she was going out to dinner with
her family and they would meet me later for a drink. She
added that they couldn't stay out very late because they
had a flight to the Bahamas to catch early the next morning. That worked well for me because I had to pick up the

boys from their mom before she left for work at 8:00 AM the next morning.

The boys and I went to dinner at 7:30 PM, and I dropped them off at their mom's house around 8:45 PM. I went home to rest and fell asleep on the couch waiting for Robin to let me know when she was finished with dinner. At 10:30 PM, Robin texted me to meet her and Mark at The Blue Martini bar in downtown Fort Lauderdale at 11:15 PM. I got up, showered, and had a quick bite to eat before heading out the door at 11:00 PM.

When I got to The Blue Martini, Robin and Mark were there with several other friends. The bar was nearly empty, so we all decided to go to Automatic Slim's, about ten minutes away. Automatic Slim's was packed, and even though one member of our party happened to be the owner, it still took us a half hour to get our tables. I sat at one table with Mark, Robin, and our friends Erica and Bruce. We talked about how much we were all looking forward to the new year; I'd just been hired for a great job with ESPN and had begun to do a lot of public relations work for the Yankees. I was hoping to get full custody of my boys and move to New York with them. I felt like I was in control of my destiny, and that things would keep falling into place.

What was supposed to be an early night turned into 2:00 AM. Robin, Mark, and Erica had gone home, and Bruce and I decided to stay a little longer. Around 3:00 AM, I told

Bruce I was leaving. He was visiting from out of town and didn't have a car, so he asked me for a ride home. As we were getting ready to leave, a few Red Sox fans wanted to buy us a shot. I finished the drink I was having, took the celebratory shot, and walked out the door. Ten minutes later, God stepped in and turned my life upside down. I would never again question the path he wanted me to take.

While driving toward the intersection of Southwest Seventh Street and Second Avenue in downtown Fort Lauderdale, my car struck the rear end of another car that had sped through a red light. I never saw it coming. I was still in shock and pulled my car to the side of the road. Bruce was okay and all I had was a bump on the head. I jumped out of the car and ran to the intersection. What I found there would change the lives of my family and the other driver's family forever.

The driver of the other car was ejected from her vehicle and was laying in the street. A young woman was standing over her. I approached and asked if she was the other driver. She said no, that the woman in the street was the driver of the other car. I asked her if they had been drinking. She replied curtly, "I don't know—she's unconscious." This is when I realized that the two women were not in the car together. As I tried to see if the injured woman was breathing, the other woman yelled at me to get away. I was nervous but still didn't think I was in any trouble. I walked back to my car to check on Bruce and get my phone. When I got there, Bruce was gone.

By that time, the police were starting to arrive at the accident site. I walked back to the intersection and told the first police officer I saw that I was the driver of the other car. We spoke briefly and walked together to my car to get my ID and insurance information. As I gave him my registration, he noticed some autographed pictures of me in my car that were left over from a recent charity event. He instantly recognized me: "You're Jim Leyritz." I replied, "Yes." He looked at my license and noticed it was my birthday. "Man, this sucks. It's your birthday and this happens."

He asked if I had been drinking and I was honest—I told him I had a few drinks. He instructed me to stand on the sidewalk while he continued to investigate. Moments later, another officer approached with more detailed questions. I explained to him that the other car went through the red light and hit me. He proceeded to tell me that the injured woman's boyfriend was on a motorcycle behind her and that he saw me go through a red light. Instinctively, I knew I was in very big trouble. My light was not red.

The officer introduced himself as Officer Buttery and told me that he was part of the DUI task force. He asked me if I had been drinking, and I repeated the same thing I told the first officer—that I had a few drinks but that I was okay. He asked me my name and I told him. He commented on my ring and asked me about it. I showed it to him and told him it was from the 1996 World Series. He proceeded with the investigation and asked me if I would take a breathalyzer test. I refused. I knew I had just finished my drink and a shot, and I was sure to test positive on the breathalyzer. He explained that he could arrest me because of my refusal. But all those years of ball playing stuck in my head: as a player, we were consistently told by management to always refuse a breath test if caught drinking and driving. Then he asked me if I would agree to do a roadside test. After going back and forth with the idea, I agreed. We went in front of his car so he could videotape my roadside test. I was nervous and scared at this point. I had never been involved in anything like this before. I took the test, and although I started early on a few things; I thought I had passed with ease. This is when my nervousness and fear turned to complete panic. He placed my arms behind my back, locked handcuffs around my wrists, and announced that he was arresting me for DUI.

He asked me if I understood what was happening, and I said, "No." Things went from bad to worse when he informed me that the other driver had died. Still in shock about being arrested, I could barely even process that news. I was still trying to figure out why I had been arrested. I felt completely in control of my faculties. As he put me in the back of the police car and slammed the door, I knew I was about to be blamed for something I didn't do.

I was charged with DUI vehicular manslaughter and was booked into the Fort Lauderdale County Jail. I was released eleven hours later after posting bail. The biggest fight of my life was just beginning.

12

Justice?

The day after the accident, everything was a blur. I hadn't slept in twenty-four hours and was staying at my ex-wife's house with the boys because a team of reporters was camped out in front of my house. Oddly enough, at the time, Karri was very supportive. The boys were scared to death, and so was I. I knew the charges against me were severe, and if found guilty, I might never see them grow up.

I went to the hospital so a doctor could check the bump on my head (which was giving me terrible headaches) and for something to help me sleep. I was diagnosed with a concussion and prescribed some anti-anxiety medicine to help me calm down. My mom and dad came down from Cincinnati and the three of us returned to my house. By then, Karri had taken the boys to stay with her to protect them from ruthless reporters (some of whom even chased my kids on their bikes).

The reporters were still outside my house and they circled like vultures, waiting to prey on anyone for a photograph or a comment. We were trapped in the house. I could barely function. All I could think about was the woman who had died and the fact that the police were blaming me.

Two attorney friends, Mike Alman and Jeff Ostrow, came to check on me. They talked to my parents and me about the importance of hiring a defense attorney as quickly as possible. Jeff suggested I speak to his good friend Mike Gottlieb who was a defense attorney. My close friends Todd Watson, Tom Cetnar, Mike Murphy, and Mitch Goldstein also came over to offer their support. Todd, through his boss's recommendation, suggested the defense attorney David Bogenschutz.

Over the next two days, we interviewed these attorneys at the house. Since I was still reeling from the accident and devastated by the charges against me, I asked my parents to decide who to hire. They chose Bogenschutz, who had a reputation as one of the best high-profile defense attorneys in Fort Lauderdale. He was particularly skilled at getting to the truth (a truth we would later learn the state would go to great lengths to cover up, even if it included hiding evidence and lying to the judge).

We now had Bogenschutz on board, and I started coping a little bit better. It really helped that my parents were with me. I had been avoiding the newspapers and local television news since the accident. I knew what people were saying about me, and I just could not watch. A friend called to tell me I was familiar with the woman who had died in the accident and that her name was Fredia Veitch. Having met her on several occasions, I had actually been out with her in a group setting just several weeks before. She was very good friends with several people I knew. I was floored. The pain and sorrow I felt was overwhelming.

A woman had died, two young children had lost a mother, and all people could talk about what the fact that I used to play baseball for the Yankees. I was sickened. I struggled desperately between remorse and anger, and I needed to speak to someone at my church. My dad took me to Flamingo Road Church where I had been a member for nearly ten years. The reporters who were camped outside my house chased us all the way there and tried to follow us in. Pastor Garland, who would later become a dear friend, kicked them out. I met with Pastor Garland and Pastor Ricky and told them everything that had happened and the severe angst I was going through. I had no idea how I was going to get through this; we prayed together for more than an hour.

Stefanie Newman, the Florida state attorney who was prosecuting me, painted a very slanted picture of me whenever she spoke about the case in the media. She portrayed me as a boozed-up lout, a crummy ex-ballplayer only interested in drinking and partying. She didn't mention a word about me being a single father who had been awarded primary custody of my three sons or that I was trying to raise them alone; nor did she mention a word about all the charity work I had done or the fact that I had never had a alcohol-related incident—ever.

In fact, Newman *knew* that these allegations about me were untrue. She and Laura, my old fiancée, used to get their nails done at the same place. Newman knew that I took Laura and her son into my home and that I was a good father, but she still wanted to portray me as a boozer. I will always believe that her prosecution of me was only to advance her own career. She needed to win a high-profile case at any cost. Lucky me.

The prosecutor had read in the *New York Post* that I was a drinker and a partier, and she tried to exploit this at every opportunity. A photograph of me that once ran in the *Post* did indeed show me partying—celebrating the Yankees' World Series victory in 1996. When I lived in New York, I did go out a lot. I went to many Broadway shows, Knicks and Rangers games, music award shows, and other events that make New York such a great place. But I was married and I had children and I was *not* an alcoholic. Nor was I a "party animal"—I was just somebody who embraced a city he had fallen in love with. I considered New York City my home away from home, and still do. At the time of the accident, those days were long gone and I had been a full-time father for more than four years. Still, I was crucified in the press and had to prove to the state that I did not have a drinking problem.

Although I had no prior history of alcohol problems of any kind, the court ordered me to be on a home Breathalyzer for two and a half months. I had to breathe into the machine three times every day to prove to the court and to the prosecutor that I was not alcohol-dependent. The machine was programmed to recognize my breath, so if anyone else breathed into it, it would not work. If the home Breathalyzer showed that I was drunk, there'd be a cop at my door within minutes.

I had never agreed to the home Breathalyzer, but on the day of my arraignment, my lawyer, David Bogenschutz, was sick and couldn't be there. He sent his associate, Mike Dutko. Newman took advantage of Dutko. When I was asked to sign the agreement to the home Breathalyzer, I told him, "Mike, this is not what I agreed to." He told me that David would take care of it. But I knew better: once it was signed, I'd be stuck with it.

The home machine went off at all hours of the day and night, and it was extremely loud. It was very disturbing and woke up the children often. Still, whenever the device called, "demanding" that I blow into it, I did. I had to pay $75 per week for this "service," and I also had to report to Pretrial Services (PTS) officer Michelle Lundy once a week; but because of various problems with the machine, I often spoke with her two or three times a week.

During a court appearance on April 1, 2008, Bogen-schutz told the presiding judge, Marc Gold, that we thought the home Breathalyzer tests—approximately 270 samples *without a single failed test*—were enough evidence to prove that I was *not* alcohol-dependent. Judge Gold agreed, and the home machine was removed. The ignition interlock device that was placed in my car was another issue. I didn't agree that I needed it, but the judge wanted to give the state something to prove that I was not a danger to society. Judge Gold said that the trial might not start for approximately six months, so he instructed Newman and Bogenshutz to draw up new orders that would remove the home Breathalyzer. The new orders stated that an ignition interlock device would be installed when I got my driver's license back the next month.

There was no language in any of the new orders, nor in any of our agreements (with the court or with the state's attorney) stating that I was not allowed to drink if I was not driving.

David instructed me to go to Pretrial Services with the new orders. My mother, who was then living with us, went with me. (My dad had gone back to Ohio right after the accident because he was having anxiety problems and his blood pressure became unmanageable.) When Michelle Lundy read the new orders, she had me sign off on the old Pretrial Services orders. She said, "Good-bye and good luck," and said that I was no longer required to call or report to her any longer. Since that day in April 2008 through February 2009, I had no contact in person, by phone, in writing, or any other way with Pretrial Services. I was not being monitored anymore.

After I left the courthouse that day, I said to my mother, "I'm buying a bottle of wine tonight to make a toast to you for staying here with me for four months and taking care of me and the boys." My mom had been with me every minute since the accident and truly was my rock and strength during this time. We shared a toast and from that point on, I assumed that if I wanted to have a glass of wine or two before bed, it was perfectly fine.

I thought the purpose of the ignition interlock device in my car was to keep me from drinking and driving, not to detect whether there was any alcohol *at all* in my system. I also had no idea that the device was highly sensitive and would trigger false-positives through traces of alcohol or certain chemicals contained in products such as mouthwash, cologne, energy drinks, and certain spices and oils. If I had, I certainly would have done a few things differently.

In the midst of trying to cope with the aftermath of the accident, prepare for my trial, and resume some sort of a

normal life for me and the boys, the interlock device created a frenzy of false accusations by the State Attorney
resulting in a series of brutal reports by the press.

On four occasions, from September of 2008 until January of 2009, the ignition interlock device showed that
I had either trace amounts of alcohol or those certain
chemicals that could trigger false-positives in my system. Each of those times, the machine emitted only a
"warning" signal but never registered over the machine's
limit (.05), which would have resulted in a "fail" signal
and shut the engine down. None of these instances were
ever cases of my drinking and then trying to drive. The
fourth occasion occurred in January when the device registered a trace amount of alcohol on my first breath but
still allowed the car to start. The device required a second breath, two minutes later (and then every five minutes thereafter) that registered over the limit (.051) and
shut down the car. It was 8:00 in the morning, and I had
obviously not been drinking. However, I had been drinking wine the night before. Unfortunately, this failed test
would have to be reported to the state attorney's office.
Knowing this, I contacted my attorney and explained to
him what had happened.

Bogenshutz was not concerned and said that it was no
big deal. He said that if Newman saw it and asked him

about it, he'd deal with it. He thought I was still being monitored by Pretrial Services. I insisted that I was not. I thought I was allowed to drink, but obviously not allowed to drink and drive—which I had never done before the accident and would never do again. David wisely advised me to quit drinking completely as long as the device was on my car, so I did. In February, Newman received a notice from the Department of Motor Vehicles (DMV) notifying her of the failed test and of my understanding that I was allowed to drink as long as I wasn't driving. She said she thought I knew better. My lawyer pointed out that there were, at most, three or four instances in which trace amounts of alcohol or suspect chemicals had been detected the morning after I had had a few drinks or used mouthwash or cologne.

Nonetheless Newman decided to make a big deal of it, so she called Pretrial Services to find out why they had not notified her earlier about my alleged violation of the interlock device. Their answer was that they had not spoken to me since April 1, 2008, the same day Michelle Lundy received the new orders and released me from their jurisdiction. Still, Newman disagreed. After further probing, it turns out Pretrial Services had screwed up. They should still have been monitoring me. Lundy read the orders incorrectly and decided that she better cover her ass, so she went behind the state's back to Judge Gold to get a warrant for my arrest for violating my bond. The judge signed the warrant. On February 9, 2009, at approximately 11:05 AM, I was staying with my friend, Mitch, in Weston, Florida, because I knew that there was a warrant out for my arrest (an acquaintance happened to work for Broward County in the warrant department and gave me a heads up) and didn't want the arrest to happen at my home in front of my kids. I was incensed. I couldn't believe that Pretrial Services were trying to cover up their mistake and actually having me arrested. The next morning, a fully armed Broward County Sheriff's Office task force (a S.W.A.T. team, as if they were capturing a terrorist or a bank robber!) arrived at Mitch's house. They surrounded the house and informed the neighbors and the pool worker that there was nothing to be worried about; they were just coming to get a famous baseball player.

I found out later that they actually said this before knocking on the door. When I answered the door, just wearing the shorts and the long-sleeve shirt I had slept in—no shoes or socks—an officer with a drawn weapon asked me to step outside. As I walked out onto the front porch, I was grabbed by another officer and surrounded by about five more—all with their guns drawn. Two other officers secured the house and the backyard.

I told the officers that the warrant wasn't valid and that my attorney and the state attorney were in front of the judge right then trying to figure things out. No one wanted to hear it. As one officer asked me to put my hands behind my back, I told him to take it easy. Apparently, that was the wrong thing to say. He pulled my left arm back with such force that it almost knocked me over. I again asked him to please take it easy—that I was not resisting arrest. At this time, I asked the pool man, who was now standing in the driveway watching it all unfold, to be my witness. I asked if he had a video camera on his cell phone. He didn't, but he agreed to stick around and watch the actions of the officers.

As the police were handcuffing me, one of the officers said, "You want cameras? We can get them here if you want." We were standing on the front porch, and I asked the officers if I could at least get a pair of sneakers so I could have a little dignity as I walked into jail. At first, he refused. But after talking to the other officers, and after my continued pleading, the officer relented and said, "Okay. I'll go and get his shoes." He asked me where they were. I told him they were on my suitcase in the guest room on the left. I had my car keys and my wallet inside my baseball cap—on top of the suitcase. I also had $400 cash in my cap.

The officer entered the house and retrieved my shoes. Of course, he removed the laces before giving them to me. He had to slip the shoes on my feet, because I was still handcuffed. We then walked down the driveway to the police cars, which were outside the four-foot-tall gate in the front of the house. I gave an officer the numeric code to open the gate but it didn't work. He tried again, but it still didn't work. I think he entered the wrong number on purpose. Then they noticed a magnetic pad on the drive-way. They asked the pool guy to drive his truck to the pad to see if it would open the gate. It didn't. The pool guy then called Mitch, the homeowner, to ask how to open the gate. He said that he was right around the corner and would be there in two minutes.

Apparently, that was not fast enough for the S.W.A.T. officers. Two guys grabbed me and they threw me over the fence, still handcuffed. (The pool guy's truck was right there. I could have stepped up on the front bumper and walked over the gate.) When they put me over the gate, they wrenched my shoulder. It was a very sharp pain, and I shouted out, "Hey, hey, hey!" Finally, they put me down. I complained about the pain, and I asked them to stop. They didn't. As we were standing on the other side, my wrists were being squeezed by the handcuffs so I asked one of the police officers to loosen the cuffs a little. He refused. They put me in a police car.

If I had been taken directly to jail, I would have seen a judge almost immediately, all this would have been cleared up, and I would have been released due to the invalid warrant that was issued by Pretrial Services. But, of course, that didn't happen. It was Friday, the start of the President's Day weekend, so I was first taken to a holding cell in Davie, then to the main jail after 5:00 PM.

When I woke up the next morning, my entire left side was numb. I went into a panic. My breathing became impossible to control. I thought this was it, that I was going to have a heart attack. I asked the officers to call my children to tell them that I loved them, and to call my ex-wife to let her know I was going to the hospital.

I was rushed to Broward General where I spent the next three days. I was tested and retested for complications of high blood pressure (which I had never had before). I was also put on morphine because of the pain in my shoulder from being thrown over the gate. After I was released from the hospital three days later and transferred back to the Broward County Jail, I was finally allowed to make a phone call. I asked Karri to pick up my car and my belongings at Mitch's house, including my keys, my wallet, and $400 that were in my cap on top of my suitcase in the guest room. She could use the $400 for the boys and herself until I got out. She called Mitch's wife, Jackie, to let her know she was coming over. As Jackie checked the room, she saw the keys in my cap and my wallet on the bed, open; but the $400 was gone. The only person in that room since my arrest was the police officer who got my shoes. Thank you, Broward County's finest.

After being incarcerated for five days, I went in front of Judge Gold. He wasn't aware that the state had asked to dismiss him from my case due to a conflict of interest (he had an issue with one of the state's expert witnesses who had lied in his courtroom in the past). The state was waiting for the appellate court to make the decision. This meant technically, Judge Gold did not have the authority to sign the warrant from Pretrial Services for my arrest. I was handcuffed to a bed with my feet shackled (like I was Charles Manson), guarded around the clock by *two* police officers for four days, sustained a shoulder injury, had four hundred dollars stolen, and endured humiliating media coverage—all because Pretrial Services made a mistake and then tried to cover it up. The state apologized to Judge Gold but never to me for what they had put me and my family through.

We then had to go in front of another judge to decide whether the orders I had been given were clear. Judge Ilona Holmes heard the case, since Gold had no jurisdiction. Judge Holmes looked at the orders and said, "I can see why Mr. Leyritz believed that the only restrictions were having a valid Florida driver's license and having the ignition interlock device installed on his car." She also pointed out that I did not have a prior record or any history of anything to do with alcohol.

She questioned the state's attorney, "How could Pretrial Services issue a warrant for Mr. Leyritz's arrest if they were not monitoring him? How could this happen?"

The state answered that Pretrial Services had made a mistake. But because this was a high-profile case in Broward County—with media in her courtroom—she chastised me.

"Mr. Leyritz," she said, "if I were you I wouldn't even have Listerine on your breath, or you're going back to jail."

I was going to respond that I had played by the rules and hadn't done anything wrong, but I bit my tongue. She was crystal clear that the new rule was that I could not have anything at all to drink. No alcohol whatsoever.

I respected that. From that day on—February 13, 2009, to the day of my verdict December 2, 2010—I did not have one single drop of alcohol—not even Listerine. But this wouldn't be the last time Stefanie Newman went after headlines.

In May 2009 at 11:30 AM, I had my weekly urine test at Pretrial Services and went back to my house to eat lunch, which consisted of some chicken wings and cupcakes. A few minutes after eating, I got into my car to pick up my son from school. Before I could start my car, I blew into the ignition interlock device as I had done thousands of times before. Surprisingly, it registered a failed test and would not let me start the car. It was locked. I immediately called the monitoring company and asked what the hell was going on: Once again, I had not had any alcohol to drink. I was pissed off. The technician asked me what I had eaten. When I told him chicken wings he laughed and said chicken wings can set off the machine, resulting in a false-positive. Whether it's the spices, the hot sauce, or some "secret ingredient," I don't know.

He instructed me to rinse my mouth out with water and to breathe again. I did, and, sure enough, my car started. I made other arrangements for my son to be picked up from school and drove straight to the ignition inter-lock device company office to have the download report pulled from the device. The download registered .057 for the initial breath that had set off the machine and locked the car. The next breath (the one I took after rinsing my mouth) registered 0.000. I asked—no, I demanded—that the company call Pretrial Services to explain that I was *not* drinking and that I had just eaten the wrong food for lunch. The PTS officer was not thrilled to get yet another phone call about me. She said that she'd still have to inform the state's attorney. I said that I was coming to her office to take another urine test to prove that I had not been drinking, which I did. I called Bogenschutz to let him know what was going on.

Again, he was nonchalant.

That night, after the incident with the machine, I was sitting on the back porch with a woman I was dating at the time. I was explaining all the craziness that had been going on that day. She was planning to take me to the emergency room so that I could get a prescription for something to settle my nerves. I was extremely agitated and very nervous that the police would throw me in jail again before I could get the results of the urine test the next morning. Almost on cue, the police arrived. They told me that they had received a 911 call from someone claiming I was suicidal.

"Excuse me?!" I exclaimed. "Are you kidding me? I'm sitting here having dinner with my girlfriend. I'm afraid that tomorrow night, you'll be back with a warrant to arrest me again, because the state's attorney is going to try to take advantage of this situation before I can explain to the judge what has happened!" Which, of course, she had done before. The police tried to calm me down and determine if I was indeed suicidal. I assured the police that I was not. But I did say that I had asked my girlfriend to take me to the hospital for some anxiety medicine.

The police told me the 911 call had come from a woman in New Jersey who said that I seemed upset. I had two choices. First, I could ask them to leave and then they would determine whether I was in danger of hurting myself. Second, they could just take me to a hospital to make sure that I got there safely. In either instance, they were required to make sure that I got the help I needed. They could not take my word that I would go to the emergency room on my own.

Naturally, I didn't want to be taken to the psych ward in jail. Nor did I want to go with them to the emergency room. I was worried about the effect this could have on my three sons who were in the house. I decided that I didn't really have many options. They put me in a police car and took me to the emergency room at Broward General. The officer driving said that he was just acting as a taxi to get me to the hospital; no report would be filed, and it would be kept quiet.

At the hospital, I was told that since I'd been brought in by the police, I had to be processed through the psych ward. I tried to explain that the police had not arrested me; they had just acted as a cab for me. I was never in police custody. Nevertheless, they made me go through the psych ward. I asked for something to help me sleep, but they told me no—only a doctor could prescribe medications, and all the doctors in the psych ward were off duty. They told me I would have to spend the night. I could not believe I was in this situation.

I didn't sleep at all. Finally, early the next morning, a nurse asked me if a doctor had seen me yet. I yelled, "NO!" I was very upset. She wrote me up as "agitated and suicidal." She said she'd be right back, but never returned. About two hours later, another nurse came in and told me I had been "Baker Acted." I asked what that meant.

In Florida, the Baker Act permits the involuntary hospitalization of people who appear to be a danger to themselves or to others. This second nurse told me that I had been written up as "belligerent." I felt like I was in *The Twilight Zone*. All I wanted was to get some medicine and go home to sleep. I begged to see a doctor. When the doctor finally arrived, he interviewed me and wrote me a prescription for Ativan (a medication that treats anxiety) before chuckling and suggesting that I get away for a while to relax.

I thought that was the end of it. But as I was getting ready to leave, one of the nurses told me that she had been getting calls from reporters and the story was all over the newspapers. The sergeant who had brought me in had decided that he wanted to see his name in print, too, so he took it upon himself to call the newspapers to report that Jim Leyritz had been acting suicidal and was taken to the psych ward for observation. Another one of Broward County's Finest.

That afternoon, a hearing was scheduled at 2:30 PM in front of Judge Gold. The results of both urine tests had already come back at 10:00 AM that morning as *negative*. The ignition interlock device company had confirmed that the results on their machine were indeed caused by spicy food and not alcohol: I had not been drinking. Bogenschutz spoke to Newman and said, "I guess there isn't any need for a hearing." But Newman (who was running for judge) decided to go forward with the hearing.

Judge Gold reviewed the paperwork and asked her tersely, "Why are we here?" If it weren't a rhetorical question, *I* would've answered, "Clearly, because the prosecution wants some more publicity before the election." Newman was trying to make my life miserable, and she was doing an excellent job.

Later that day, Newman left a message on Bogenschutz's cell phone that said, "Hey, David, why don't we go out for chicken wings?" When I heard that, I was floored. After everything my boys and I had been through, I couldn't believe that she had the audacity to make a joke of it, especially to my own attorney. I thought that was in very poor taste.

My car was still impounded. I had not had a drink for more than a year. My trial had been delayed numerous times. Every time I got behind the wheel of my car, I had to breathe into the ignition interlock device (which cost me

$75 per month) and was required to submit urine samples every week. Between all the court-ordered tests, meetings with my attorneys, and driving the boys to and from school and sports, it was almost impossible for me to find a job.

My case was originally supposed to go to trial in May 2008. It was rescheduled for March 2009. I was devastated. I had hoped and prayed that this would all be over by April 2009, so I could go back to work when the baseball season started. I had lost all means of income because of the accident. MLB.com, ESPN, and the Yankees all held me at a distance and wanted to wait until after the trial before committing to any contracts with me. My life was literally on hold. I spent my days taking care of the boys and poring over depositions and evidence that I would later need to clear my name. The delays became agonizing.

March came and went, and the criminal trial was postponed again. In the meantime, I decided to resolve a civil lawsuit, which the family of the other driver filed against me shortly after the accident. My attorneys in that case, Jeff Ostrow and John Richards, explained to me that the burden of proof in a civil matter is far less than in a criminal case. Although I did not cause or contribute to the accident because I did not run the red light, the fact that I was driving might be enough for a civil jury to hold me partially responsible. They advised me to settle out of court. I respected their advice, and I agreed for two reasons: First, I wanted the children of the other driver to receive the insurance money, and second, I did not want the children publicly exposed to some damaging details about their mother and father's personal life. All of the children—hers and mine—had already been through so much. In retrospect, despite the outcome of the criminal case, I am happy with my attorneys' advice and my decision to follow it.

More than a year later, in the middle of my case, Judge Gold was transferred from the criminal branch of the court to the civil branch. But when he transferred, he decided to keep only one case: mine. He was required to take a course to brush up on civil law, which now meant the trial date had to be delayed again.

The prosecutor's schedule changed too. By May 2010, she still couldn't try the case because her daughter had a bat mitzvah, and she said that she needed *an entire month* to prepare. She couldn't do it in June either because she had a family vacation planned. Two weeks before the trial was set to finally start on July 12, 2010, the judge noticed an error. He had written the wrong date on his calendar. An emergency hearing was held and the judge insisted, "We are going on the nineteenth." But again, this interfered with another one of the prosecutor's vacations, which she told the judge she had planned with five other couples. She simply could not change the date. The judge set the date yet again for September 20, 2010. So as

I sold everything I owned to provide for me and my boys, and even borrowed money from friends and family just to get by, the state's attorney was busy planning parties and social events. What a joke.

The previous summer, my ex-wife was evicted from her apartment and lost her job. She was no longer able to take the boys on her scheduled days. This created a problem for me, as I had found some much-needed work up in New York signing autographs at trade shows and needed to be able to travel. Karri and I were in a fairly decent place and were at least civil to one another. The boys begged me not to let their mom be homeless. I had been deeply involved in my church ever since the accident and decided that helping her was the right thing to do, if not for her, then at least for the boys. I offered her a room in my house for three months so she could find work and get back on her feet. But only under the condition that she changed her lifestyle while she lived under my roof.

The first month went okay. She was going to meetings and helping out with the boys and around the house. The second month things changed. She started staying out late at night and sometimes wouldn't even come home. This caused the boys to worry, and I started to regret that I had offered her the room. Things were stressful enough for the boys and me as we waited for trial, and I didn't need any more headaches.

In June, I asked her to start looking for a new place to live. She still wasn't working and her partying was becoming more and more frequent. She refused to leave and said she had no place to go. A few days after that, I pulled up my bank statement on the computer and noticed that there was money missing from one of my accounts. Karri had stolen a check from my business account and forged my signature. I was insulted and disgusted, as were the boys. After giving her a place to live and trying to help her, she blatantly stole from me.

I left the house without even talking to her. I texted her: "Please get your stuff and move out. You are no longer welcome in my home."

Her reply was "F--- you. You will have to evict me."

I contacted my attorney to start the eviction process and texted her that the eviction was underway. That night, the boys and I went to sleep around midnight. The next thing I knew, at 2:45 AM there were two police officers knocking on my front door. Still half-asleep, I was handcuffed and told they were arresting me for domestic battery. Another bump in the road.

Karri had gotten drunk, somehow inflicted injury on herself (a small cut above her eye), and blamed it on me. She had told the police three different stories and none of them added up. Even the officer at the scene told his sergeant that he didn't think anything had happened. Still, the sergeant on duty said it was protocol to bring in the uninjured party. That would be me.

This incident couldn't have happened at a worse time. We were two weeks away from starting the trial, and I was on the brink of finally being able to clear my name and get back to work. Karri's latest stunt would not only hurt me in the media, but now threatened to impact a potential jury pool. The press had a field day. I had always had a thick skin, but the latest stories circulating about me were taking a heavy toll on my faith. I ended up spending twelve days in jail waiting to prove Karri's latest accusations were totally false.

Those twelve days were filled with emptiness and despair. I could not figure out why God would, once again, take me away from my children and drag my name through the mud for something He knew I didn't do. As much as I felt sorry for myself, I spent a great deal of that time thinking about my sister's husband Joe, who was battling ALS, and the woman who had passed away in the accident. I knew the situation I was in was only temporary and tried to reassure myself that God had a plan for me.

After eight days of testimony from police officers and witnesses, Judge Gold ruled that he believed the domestic violence incident never occurred and allowed me free on my original bond. To my surprise, he also ruled that I was not allowed to go back to my own house since Karri was still living there. He made me find other accommodations for the boys and me. This made absolutely no sense; I was the one paying the bills and she wasn't even on the lease. To make matters worse, before I could get all of my belongings, she proceeded to steal anything that was of value from my house. Unbelievable.

After the boys and I found a new place to live, I vowed to never have any contact with their mother again. Subsequently, I was advised by the police that any time I was in her presence I needed to have an officer present. I simply could not afford to have my freedom jeopardized ever again because of her false allegations. (In March 2011, Mike Gottlieb, the attorney I mentioned earlier, finally got the domestic battery charge thrown out of court due to insufficient evidence.)

13

Redemption

Once the boys and I were settled into our new house, I swore that from that point on I would not date or get involved with anyone. This latest incident had ruined another budding relationship, and I was not willing to involve anyone else in this mess. I began working more and more at the church and spent a lot of time with the boys. I focused on fighting my case and trying to finally put all of this behind me. The trial was just two weeks away.

But wait, Groundhog Day. Another delay. But this time, the delay was actually regarding something in our favor. Bogenschutz had found a video that the state attorney knew existed but had not entered into evidence. The video would prove the accident happened twelve minutes earlier than the state attorney was claiming. This was integral to our defense for several reasons: It confirmed the timing of the accident, which coincided with the woman's cell phone records. This proved that the crash may have happened at the exact time the woman was being bombarded with phone calls and text messages from her husband, who had been waiting for her to come home.

These phone calls and text messages would also explain why she may have been distracted enough to run the red light. The video was also critical because it showed a discrepancy as to what my blood-alcohol content (BAC) was at the time of the accident. The blood tests taken three hours after the crash showed .14, which according to our defense expert, meant I was .06 at the time of the accident. The state was trying to claim that my BAC was as high as a .198 (comatose). The last drink and shot I had as I walked out of the bar would not have had time to impair me at the new time of the accident. (It takes approximately forty-five minutes to an hour for an average person to be impaired by the last drink they had.) This was a huge break in my case.

When this was presented to the judge, he asked the state, "How could such an important piece of evidence not be revealed until two years later?" He was visibly upset (and would later impose sanctions on the state for hiding it). Bogenschutz needed time to review the tape and figure out how it would bolster our defense. When he did, he discovered that the state, or the police, had destroyed some crucial evidence that was also on the tape. The case was delayed indefinitely.

Up to this point, Major League Baseball had been taking care of all of the household bills for me and the boys through a remarkable charitable division called the Baseball Assistance Team (BAT). The division was headed by Jim Martin. Jim had met me shortly after my arrest and heard my story. He put his faith in me and asked the board if they would give me a grant. None of the money granted was used for my legal defense: it was only to provide a roof above our heads and food on our table. But now, after more than two years of waiting to go to trial, the grant money was running out. Without the money from BAT, I would lose everything. I had no other means of taking care of the boys. Jim talked the board into giving me a few more months, so the little bit of money I had been making in signings and appearances could be used to pay my attorneys. To me, this BAT extension was another sign from God encouraging me to keep moving forward.

I went to church that Sunday and thanked God. I

also prayed that when all this was over, he would bring a Christian woman into my life. I wanted a companion who I could share my faith with, and I also wanted the boys to see what a healthy, loving, and God-based relationship looked like. At that time, their mom was only seeing them two or three days a month, even though she lived a few miles away. I just wanted to get everything over with and get back to raising a healthy and happy family. I prayed 2010 would be the year for my redemption.

While waiting for the trial, I had already missed Old Timers Day at the end of the Yankees' 2008 season—the last one at the old Yankee Stadium—and the final game ever played there. Because the case was still pending, I was not invited to any of the ceremonies or festivities. This hurt, but I still attended as a fan. With the latest trial delay, I wouldn't be invited to the opening of the new Yankee Stadium either. This was devastating. I would not be a part of the one stadium that held my most-beloved memories and historic moments nor would I be a part of the new stadium and latest Yankee dynasty, which my homerun had helped build.

Still, I was determined to see it. My friend Todd called me and said, "I am taking you to New York and you are not missing this day." That trip would wind up being the one trip to New York that would change my personal life forever. The woman that I had been praying for, who was supposed to come into my life *after* the trial, quietly entered right in the middle of it.

Todd and I were having dinner on April 16, 2009, at
Elaine's, one of my favorite restaurants in the city, owned
by an amazing woman and devoted Yankee fan whom I
consider my "New York Mom." The front of the bar was
standing room only, and I noticed a very beautiful woman
waiting for a table. I asked her if she and her friend would
like to sit down while they were waiting. They did. Her
name was Michelle, and she was a California girl in New
York on business. She knew nothing about baseball and,
therefore, nothing about me (thank God). When I mentioned I was there for Opening Day, she replied, "What's
opening?"

After two hours of conversation, she never left for her
own table. We talked about life and family, and at some
point, she noticed that I hadn't been drinking. She asked
me why. I was very hesitant to explain all of what I was
going through—she had no idea who I was—so I just said
I didn't drink. It happened to be her birthday so I went up
to the bar and asked Alex, one of the bartenders who I
had known for many years, to bring her a glass of cham-
pagne. When Alex came over to the table, it was obvious
that she knew him too; he gave her a hug and wished her
a happy birthday.

The night was winding down and I asked her and
her friend to join us at my friend Mark's bar down the
street. She agreed and the four of us jumped into a cab.
As we walked into the bar, a group of friends and fans

who hadn't seen me since the accident started screaming, "Welcome back, King!" and giving me hugs and high-fives. This took Michelle by surprise.

Puzzled, she looked at her friend Trisha and grabbed my arm. "Who are you?" she asked. This is where I thought she would turn around and run.

I pulled Michelle aside and told her everything. She listened intently, and when I got to the part about the accident, she stopped me and announced, "You live in Florida!"

It turns out, Alex (the bartender at Elaine's) had told Michelle about me the year before. She was getting out of a long and difficult marriage, and he had mentioned that he thought the two of us would make a nice couple. (Apparently, she laughed it off at the time.) We talked about how I was coping with all of the pressures, and I told her that a book called *The Purpose Driven Life* had been my saving grace.

Her face went pale and she replied wryly, "Yes. I know it well, and love it too. It was written by my pastor."

Although we hit it off and spent the next few nights going out to dinner, taking walks, and enjoying the city, I just could not bring myself to start another relationship. I told myself Michelle would just be someone who I could see once in a while and maybe meet up with during my travels.

When I returned to Florida, I tried to put her out of my mind and concentrate on my case. But by September,

I was still thinking about her. I gave her a call and invited her to meet me in New York for the playoffs. The Yankees were playing the Angels. She turned me down, saying she was busy running her business and taking care of Ava and Isabella, her two young daughters. We began talking on a more regular basis, almost every night. Our conversations went from flirty banter to deep and meaningful discussions about all that we had lost, what we had learned as a result, and how we both wanted to spend the future giving back and making the world a better place. We had a lot of the same values and were both committed to putting God first in our life.

I really wanted to see her again so I made her a bet I knew I couldn't lose: If the Yanks won the series, she would have to come visit me, and if the Angels won, I would come visit her. It was a good time and a great place to settle a bet.

Of course, the Yankees won. With my trial still delayed, God stepped in and got me a job in Arizona the following month. It was Moose Skowron and Hank Bauer's Fantasy Camp. This camp is designed for men over thirty-five who want to live out their fantasy to play baseball for the New York Yankees. At the camp they spend a week playing on a "Yankee" team that is coached by real former Yankee legends who act as the coaches. I was one of the coaches. I called Michelle and asked her to meet me in Arizona. She accepted. I felt like a little kid in high school again. I hadn't seen her in five months, and although we had spent countless hours on the phone, I didn't know how I would feel about seeing her again. As soon as I walked into the hotel lobby and saw her face, I knew I was in trouble. I can't exactly say it was love at first sight (this was the second time I saw her), but it felt that way.

We spent five beautiful days together. When she left, we talked seriously about trying to forge a long-distance relationship. It was November, and with the trial starting in December, we knew the odds were stacked against us. There was so much uncertainly in both of our lives (she was still making the adjustment to being divorced and was focused on her girls' emotional well-being). But we both wanted to give it a shot.

We continued talking on the phone every night for at least one hour and to this day have never missed a call. God had brought us into each other's lives just as we both had prayed, when we needed each other most. The distance allowed each of us to tend to our individual needs and to those of our children. He would bring us together every two to three weeks to deepen our bond and give one another strength. The path God created for us was not conventional, but it was working.

The problem was, I still had to face a manslaughter trial that could put me in prison for up to fifteen years. Michelle had reviewed all of the depositions, witness statements, and police reports early on; it was obvious to her that I had not run the red light. Still, ours was a justice system that wasn't always just, and the uncertainty of six jurors determining my fate was terrifying. Michelle made her decision and told me she would stand by me. She had grown to know and love my boys and wanted to give them some stability in the midst of chaos. These boys had been through so much.

After years of postponements, I finally had my day in court. I was somewhat relieved to learn that Judge Gold hadn't been recused from the case after all. The trial started on November 1, 2010. It started off with a big blow, one we hadn't seen coming. The judge had decided to suppress the facts that the woman driving the other car had a BAC of .18, was texting while driving, and was not wearing a seatbelt. Bogenschutz was livid, and I was shocked that the jury would hear only half the truth.

I thought of hiring a public relations company to report the facts of the case that I knew weren't getting reported to the press. It was a smear campaign all over again, but my mind was eased a bit when I found out that TruTV's *In Session* was covering the trial, and that Beth Karas was assigned to cover it. She was a former prosecuting attorney from New York City and knew both sides of every situation—in the courtroom and out—and I trusted that she was unbiased in her reporting. She and her colleagues did a tremendous job of zeroing in on the facts and getting them out there in a straightforward and no-nonsense way.

Despite the enormous hurdles, David Bogenschutz was brilliant. The way he commanded the courtroom and worked the jury was masterful. His attention to detail and knowledge of the case laws was exceptional. We spent countless hours going over depositions and facts surrounding the case, and we worked tirelessly with experts Ken Bynum and Stephen Rose to try to determine where the state thought they had a case. One of our primary objectives was to figure out how we could get the suppressed evidence to the jury. We had no idea how we could do it without risking the possibility of a mistrial.

Lucky for us, a bold and slick cross-examination by Bogenschutz and a haphazard cross-examination by Newman invited evidence of the other driver's BAC and lack of seatbelt use right back into the courtroom. Judge Gold was so upset with Newman's mistake in her cross-examine that he cleared the courtroom. Remember, Judge Gold had ruled in favor of the state after it had spent six months fighting for this evidence to be inadmissible. Newman was now deemed ever so politely by the press as "an asleep at the wheel prosecutor." Justice was finally being served.

The trial lasted eighteen painful days. Before the jury even began deliberating, the judge dismissed one of the two felony manslaughter counts (the one based on impairment) against me. The jury, comprised of five men and one woman, began their deliberations on November 18,

2010. Those two days dragged on like years for my family, friends, and me. We sat in the courtroom the entire first day, which was Friday, November 19, and no decision was reached. It was gut-wrenching. We went home crushed and spent the entire night pacing, crying, and praying. We were terrified of a hung jury, which would mean that we would have to do this entire ordeal all over again.

Early Saturday morning we got up and got dressed for court. Michelle had received an e-mail video from her pastor, Rick Warren, about believing in hope and faith. She came out into the living room and told me and my mom that we needed to watch this message. We gathered around the computer and watched Rick explain that it wasn't just good enough to hope for something. You had to have faith and believe that it *would* happen. We all held hands and said a prayer that the jury would reach a fair decision and that they would see through any smoke and mirrors that the state tried to create. With that we headed off to court.

On Saturday, November 20, the jury continued to deliberate. When they hadn't reached a decision within the first couple of hours, we took a break. The bailiff, Brian, told us we could go out for food but instructed us not to go far. Fifteen minutes later, he called my cell phone to say the jury had reached their verdict.

The walk from the restaurant back up to the court-room seemed like the *Green Mile*. As Brian began to read the verdict, the court officer approached me from behind and quietly placed me in handcuffs. I started to get a sinking feeling until she whispered to me, "These will be off in a minute." I was totally confused and looked at my mom who had sheer panic in her eyes. Brian read the verdict.

All I heard was "Guilty" and my heart sank.

Then he continued, "of the misdemeanor charge of driving under the influence, first-time offense." I almost fell off my chair. With tears in my eyes, I thanked God and turned to David, who had done so much more than I could ever repay. This man gave me my freedom and believed in me. I gave him a giant hug before I went over and kissed my mom and my girlfriend Michelle.

The courtroom began to clear, and I went to thank three of the jurors who stayed after to talk to me and the media. It was the first time I was able to speak since the trial began. *In Session's* correspondent Beth Karas said she had never seen a jury stay after a case and shed tears for the defendant. The jurors told me they had only taken forty-five minutes to acquit me on the manslaughter charge. I joked that I wished I would have known that during the two days they had spent deliberating.

Sharon Wessinger, the sole female juror, told me she wanted to acquit me on all charges. She was adamant that she did not think I could have been over the legal limit (.08) at the time of the accident. She finally gave in and agreed to the driving under the influence (DUI) charge so that neither family would have to endure the possibility of a mistrial.

On December 2, 2010, with my mother, my two older sons, and four of the former jurors in the courtroom to support me, Judge Gold sentenced me to a $500 fine, fifty hours of community service, and one year probation. Having four of the jurors at my sentencing hearing was unprecedented. They wanted to publically demonstrate that they believed I was unjustly accused by the state. After the sentencing was imposed, I jumped up, hugged my family, and hugged David Bogenschutz again. We had been a remarkable team; and throughout the trial, I spent a great deal of time passing David notes and relaying pertinent information for him to use. Even the judge commented before the sentencing that he had never before seen a defendant so actively involved in his own defense.

My legal and emotional nightmares were over. Everyone impacted by this tragedy now had a chance to start to heal from all of the damage that was done. Not a day will go by that I don't say a prayer for the young mother who lost her life and her innocent children who will forever be without their mom. My decision to get behind the wheel that night after drinking alcohol will forever be one of the most costly mistakes I have ever made. Whether it is one drink or ten, drinking and driving is hazardous and opens all of us up to unforeseeable consequences. I will spend the rest of my life speaking out against the dangers of drinking and driving.

My mom lived with me during the entire trial. She and my boys never left my side. My brother Mike came in from Cincinnati and my friends Sergio and Larry flew down from New York. These guys were the few friends from New York who didn't turn their backs on me when the going got tough. Serge's and Larry's loyalty even included putting together a fundraiser to collect money for my defense. (I can't list everyone who came to that dinner, but I am taking this opportunity to express a heartfelt thank you).

My friends from Fort Lauderdale were there for me every step of the way, even opening themselves up to the media as "character witnesses" to shed light on the man and father they knew. Two of my former teammates, Joe Girardi and David Cone, also stood by me. My partner Michelle was my guardian angel and never stopped providing unconditional love and inspiration.

The head pastor at Potential Church, Troy Gramling, was instrumental in giving me the strength to get through these events. Our weekly meetings taught me that God sometimes allows us to pass through painful experiences that we would never choose or want. Yet when we go through them, accept them, and learn from them, our faith grows deeper. *The Purpose Driven Life*, written by Pastor Rick Warren, also saved my life. It taught me that in the midst of trouble, never ask, "Why me?" Instead ask, "What do you want me to learn?" Then trust God, and keep doing what is right.

Despite catching a lot of heat, everything worked out, but not without a tremendous amount of faith and perseverance. I have written this book for my fans and readers who have been down on their luck or just need a little inspiration for getting through the tough times. If you feel like you are always coming from behind or having to fight for a front-row seat, I hope you have been encouraged by my experiences and faith, because I sure know what it's like to come from behind.

I don't think I have ever learned any deep, lasting life-changing lessons on the crest of success. I have learned very little from winning, but I have learned a great deal from losing. I became a hero in 1996, only to find myself fighting my way out of subsequent hardships. Such is the game of life. There's a hero inside of each of us, and the journey toward peace of mind and acceptance for both the good and the bad that happen in life is a journey that I now offer to you as you round each base of your own life and try to find your best route home—safe.

Acknowledgments

From Jim Leyritz:

I'd like to start by thanking God first and foremost. As my journey took me in and out of faith, He stood by and triumphed in the end. He is the center of my life today.

I want to thank many people who not only inspired me on my journeys, but supported me and made me believe that my dreams could come true. First and foremost, my immediate family: My mom and dad, my sister Lori, and my brother Mike. Without them, there would have been no chance for me to achieve these goals. Thank you for your love, support, and sacrifices.

My high school coach John Basalysa, my summer

coaches Joe Hayden and Frank Leo, and college coaches Robert Sapp and Keith Madison. All were very important coaches along the way to finally getting a shot at professional baseball. Doug Melvin and Bill Livsey for scouting me at a college league tournament, giving me the shot that I couldn't get through the draft, and signing me to the Yankees. There were too many coaches and players throughout the minors to name, but Joe Datin, you know why I thank you. These people inspired me to believe I could play professional baseball.

There were so many others who were supportive and sacrificed along the way (I apologize if I have left anyone out). Jeff Ostrow, Mike Alman, Mike Gottlieb, Mike Murphy, Donna Pajor, Andi Armaganian, Debbi Nicolosi, Harvey Winston, Andrew Levy, Jennifer McPhaul, Barb Leo and Gina and Lindsey, Adam Katz and Tom Reich, Mark Gilliam, Burk Showalter, Steve Sax, Dave LaPoint, Joe Girardi, David Cone, Laura Lema and Jagger, Larry Schwiger, Todd and MonicaWatson, Mitch and Jackie Goldstein, Janie and Don Tetro, Genene Nagy and Garnette, Jiff, Chris Stacio, Rick O'Shea, and all my sons' little league coaches. Pastor Garland, Pastor Ricky, Flamingo Road Prayer Group, Raul and Heather, Jeff and Melissa. Beth Karas, Steve and Sharon Wessinger, Brian Haul, and all of the members of the jury.

Now some people I must single out. George Steinbrenner, who gave me the honor of always being part of his Yankee

Family. Don Mattingly, my best teammate ever, and Pete Rose, my boyhood idol who taught me to play the game with heart and soul. Pastor Troy Gramling, my spiritual guide and the reason my faith is as evolved as it is today. David Bogenschutz, the greatest defense attorney ever, and someone who became a good friend over a very traumatic time of my life. The Baseball Assistance Team (BAT), who provided for my family.

Jeffrey and Doug Lyons for collaborating on this project. My literary agent Karen Gantz-Zahler, and my editor Michele Matrisciani, and everyone at HCI Books for telling my story.

Larry Davis and Sergio Sanchez, Team Leyritz—thanks guys, for staying true friends through all of this.

Michelle Caruso, who is my future and the best partner a man could ever hope for. Thank you, Michelle, for standing by me and believing God has great plans for us.

Finally, my three boys, Austin, Dakota, and Phoenix—who mean everything to me. You are my greatest accomplishments, and I am so proud of each of you. You have been through so much. . . . The legacy lives with you.

From Douglas B. Lyons:

When I read books in which the author thanks numerous people for help with this "project," I always wonder: What "project"? It's just a book.

Now I know better. This book has *been* a project. It didn't just happen, and it would not have happened without the work of Jim Leyritz, my brother Jeffrey (who finally got to write a book with a former Red Sox player), our indefatigable agent Karen Gantz Zahler, our patient editor Michele Matrisciani, David Vincent, and Tim Wiles, director of research at the National Baseball Hall of Fame and Museum. My thanks to all.

From Jeffrey Lyons:

My thanks go to Jim Leyritz for asking us to join him in this monumental task. The fact that he played briefly for the Boston Red Sox made it even easier! Thanks also to my brother Douglas for his tireless work, to Michele Matrisciani, and to Michelle Caruso for her contributions and perspective.

my has never shied from the ramifica- of anything he's said done," said Buck alter. "I respect that. ritz, 29, has at- ted this season to er his behavior. He shimmies his hips and his bat between y pitch but he is no and swagger Yankee veter- ation, that he A 44.

the season. This after he needed to hit .379 to merely make the team in spring and start the season as a platoon DH.

A wave of Yankee injuries struck. Showalter installed Leyritz as the cleanup hitter when Danny Tartabull went down. In the nine games since, a span in which the

bout guys promoted got to the tz swag- ium. He vening. ke the ng on as if he ible," says Jim Leyri But h

Torey Lovullo got a ticket to the Bronx before the cowboy. Leyritz wasn't going anywhere. So he opened that mouth again. And the Yankees suspended him. "They tried to make me invis-

oozes with confide

night long." And think about pr one wrong. Jim Leyritz seer

Leyritz Puts His Bat W

By JENNIFER FREY

The day he made the major leagues, Jim Leyritz called his father. Don Leyritz did not say congratula- tions. He did not say, "I'm proud of you." He told his son, succinctly, "to go out there and do something." He expected him to make an immediate impact, he expected him to produce. e thing. He

TIMES UNION *** Alban

A-C's opener wor

By Paul Schwartz

ff writer with a triple

" It's always fun wh

Leyritz swings, he puts hurt on oppon

lot of teams he could walk in and erstart on."

d for Ley wanted h iately, f, perha her way ence w young players to their turn. y's been here awhile Showalter said. "He's ned himself as a guy capa- helping the club. He's a worker. He's certainly the respect of his peers. think he's matured some." ore the 1992 seaso ich Ley

swagger, he still wears designer sun- glasses and brims with self-confi- dence. But that does not bother the Yankees because he has earned their respect. The proof is in the numbers that easily back Leyritz's self-pro-

By Paul Schwartz
Staff writer

COLONIE — The Albany-Colonie Yankee services of catcher Jim Levri beaned by Pittsfield

Leyritz was in the sixth inn and needed six

ng day marred by

Le de

plate, les

Leyritz gets big hit for A-C

By Paul Schwartz
Staff writer

GLENS FALLS — How toug Leyritz?

As tough as this: The day aft hit in the face by a pitch, he w play again.

So, it should come Leyritz was condit suddenly because

Four Named To League

Four Forest Hills bas- keteers have been named to the American Division All-Star Basketball first a fifth made

ilton County Suburban Athletic Association.

Anderson senior Joe Deeds, Anderson juniors Tim Ferguson and Jo

198
pin
ree
me

Turpin Cat

BY MICHAEL PAOLERCIO
Sports Reporter

A little book-learning can go a long way. just ask Jim Leyritz. The Turpin catcher entered this week first among the city's batting leaders with a .001 714 average (20 of 28 at bats)

Leyritz

By Paul Schwartz
Staff writer

PITTSFIELD, Mass. was the reason the Yankees had to spend a se the freezing cold Tuesd str

Yet it was Tirado w being slapped followi inning, 5-4 Eastern L over the Pittsfield Cul

Contradiction? pitched six innings o relief. If not for the hander, Jim Leyri been able to drive with a line single in

o recor

nk they respect h d Buck Showalter ritz.

Showalter even wo viewed th 3 catcher suddenly because

23	0
111	2
70	0

Merrill could not playing, didn't perfo ularly memorable statement type player." Merrill was cri he almost certainly wouldn't

Showalter, who was Ley Fort Lauderdale in 1987 and with the temperamental play me, he has seen my ups and my downs."

While the Vankees were attempting to i

Leyritz tu

By MOSS KLEIN

SEATTLE — During spring training, Buck Showalter repeat- bdly discussed the value of versatility, the importance of having use- ul players on the bench who would be ready to follow through with ris maneuvers.

Among the players the Yankees manager had in mind was Jim u eyritz, but he had doubts about him — with too many flaws. He

OF sw

s

Albany, N.Y., Sunday, April 10, 1988   D-11

D-8   SUND

"Just doing my

D-11

UNION ***